SpringerBriefs in Sociology

More information about this series at http://www.springer.com/series/10410

Blahoslav Kraus · Leona Stašová ·
Iva Junová

Contemporary Family Lifestyles in Central and Western Europe

Selected Cases

Blahoslav Kraus
University of Hradec Králové
Hradec Králové, Czech Republic

Leona Stašová
University of Hradec Králové
Hradec Králové, Czech Republic

Iva Junová
University of Hradec Králové
Hradec Králové, Czech Republic

This book is published by the financial support of the Faculty of Education, University of Hradec Králové.

ISSN 2212-6368   ISSN 2212-6376   (electronic)
SpringerBriefs in Sociology
ISBN 978-3-030-48298-5   ISBN 978-3-030-48299-2   (eBook)
https://doi.org/10.1007/978-3-030-48299-2

This Springer imprint is published by the registered company Springer Nature Switzerland AG
The registered company address is: Gewerbestrasse 11, 6330 Cham, Switzerland

The authors would like to thank Dr Liudmyla Pankiv from the Dragomanov National Pedagogical University to her contribution to this book

Foreword

Family has been in the history of society and shall undoubtedly be a topic of interest of psychology, sociology, demography, pedagogy and anthropology and other further fields in future. It is not a coincidence, because is important and in many ways an essential social group, institution, environment where everyone was brought up, which in some forms guides us throughout the life up to its very end.

Family has been a central category of this monograph, which was created within a project "Development and Support of the Multidisciplinary Scientific and Research Team for the Study of Contemporary Family at the UHK", where "Lifestyle of the Contemporary Family" was one of the topics. A research based on the topic was implemented within the framework of the project. The research had an international feature, and based on a cooperation with foreign colleagues, it was made not just only in the Czech Republic, but also in Slovakia, Ukraine, Germany, Poland and Latvia. The research set a goal to find out how contemporary families live in those countries. This gave us a number of valuable data that made it possible to compare lifestyle of those countries. The results of this research create as well essential part of this monograph.

According to the fact that the concept of lifestyle is very broad, we focused on these following areas of family lives: (a) socio-economic situation of families (employment, financial situation and a standard of living associated with it) and satisfaction in the family (what influences it), (b) leisure time (its amount, a way of spending it, use of leisure time offers), (c) media in the family lives (what type of media outweighs and who uses them).

Individual chapters correspond to this intention. Chapter 1 introduces the contemporary family in terms of changes, which had undergone in the last decades, characterises the contemporary family, its concept and issues, which is family facing these days. Furthermore there is a review about researches of families in recent time in this section and consequently there is described a project which was implemented by the research team.

Chapter 2 consists of eight parts, where individual authors try to create a picture of the contemporary family in individually monitored countries from different points of view.

Chapter 3 states research results, which deal with the family satisfaction, its affects and how it is perceived by individual countries. The socio-economic situation of contemporary families in monitored countries has been also compared.

Chapter 4 describes what role plays leisure time in the lives of contemporary families in terms of quantitative and qualitative research based on current researches, mainly the research which had been implemented by the team of authors.

Similarly, Chap. 5 is dedicated to media in the family. Firstly, it deals with media of the contemporary theory and research in general, then it describes its role in the lives of contemporary families and based on the results of our research it analyses the frequency and way of use, and how they are perceived and they enter into families' leisure time.

The aim of the team of authors is to contribute with this publication containing current knowledge both on the theoretical and on the empirical levels on the given topic and believes that it will be useful for all who are interested in this issue.

Blahoslav Kraus
University of Hradec Králové
Hradec Králové, Czech Republic

Contents

Chapter 1
A Look at the Contemporary Family's Life

Abstract This introductory chapter approaches two basic categories of the whole monography which is a family and a lifestyle. The first subchapter deals with the complexity around the definition of the term family nowadays and difficulties with its definition. Furthermore, there is a description of post-war family development in Europe up to now, changes of the functions and further changes in the families' lives differentiated in Western and Eastern part. It turns out that changes in society have caused significant changes in family lives (democratization, individualism, pluralism of family forms, dynamization, adaptability). The term lifestyle, as different concepts, is depicted in the next part of this chapter. It is perceived as a concept of multidimensional and multidisciplinary. The second subchapter contains several researches related to lives of the families. The project of our research and its goals, methods, selected sample (in total of 2437 respondents) and research process is described in the conclusion of the whole chapter.

Keywords Family · Family changes · Lifestyle · Leisure · Healthy lifestyle · Family research · Research project

1.1 Contemporary Family and Its Lifestyle

This chapter brings a view at the family development in Europe in the last sixty years and describes basic changes which the family has undergone. These are changes of demographic nature (marriage rates, marriage age, birth rate, first birth age), in family functions, in man's and woman's role and division of labour in the family. Basic processes, which characterize this post-war development, are democratization, individualism, dynamization and pluralization of family structures and forms.

The family's lifestyle is characterized as a category reflecting these changes. There are described features of lifestyle, its forms, typology and its relations to the quality of life, with healthy behaviour and also factors which contribute to formation of the family lifestyles in the contemporary postmodern society.

The situation of contemporary family is complicated. There are even arguments that today's family is internally so transformed or so vague that continued usage of the term "family" is problematic not only terminologically, but mostly socially. It

© The Author(s) 2020

B. Kraus et al., *Contemporary Family Lifestyles in Central and Western Europe*, SpringerBriefs in Sociology, https://doi.org/10.1007/978-3-030-48299-2_1

seems the idea of family has been losing its meaning and is now outdated; a question presents itself whether it was more appropriate to take a household as a basic unit or if it were better to adopt the notion of "cohabitation". It is in this context the term "family" is understood *"as a variant of intimate relational systems that can consists of intergenerational as well as intergenerational constellations (groups) of people"* (Schneewind 1998, p. 26). This definition also includes unmarried couples. Such a situation is a result of past development of family in the last decades.

Remarkably, Evelyne Sullerot provides a perspective of *post-war development of European families* consisting of three stages family went through. One could assume that differences will arise among countries divided by the Iron Curtain and that the existing distinctions will become more pronounced. However, the exact opposite happened. At the end of the 1940s in Sweden, a new "model" of family emerged and subsequently spread throughout Europe. European families experienced an almost universal rejuvenation that brought their members closer together (Sullerot 1998). Two basic trends appeared: the number of marriages increased greatly, while age at marriage decreased markedly. The difference between urban and countryside populations is not significant.

In the following years, the position and importance of family weakened due to the attempts of socially oriented societies to assume at least partially some of family's traditional functions, to provide for their citizens in case of disease, old age and unemployment, and to influence more significantly the process of upbringing as well. According to Sullerot, the primary cause of these changes lied in a profound change of values and social morality. In her view, an individual replaced family as the basic unit of society; also, because of emancipation, regardless of sex. As a consequence, in the following years there was a great decrease in marriage rate as well as birth rate, and an increase in divorce rate. Since the end of the 1970s, Swedes have taken pride in their role as teachers of modernity to the world, and they have claimed the "Sambo" option, i.e. partner cohabitation, allowed for a "happier marriage" with a lower divorce rate (Sullerot 1998).

However, further development has showed the very opposite to be true. Unmarried cohabitation breaks up more often than marriages, which leads to an increase of children born out of wedlock and of single mothers. According to U. Beck, the collision between love, family and individual freedom has become the basic characteristic and at the same time the basic problem of family. The modern society is a society of individuals, not families; therefore, the claim family is a basic unit of society loses its validity (Beck 1986). A growing number of young people perceive family as a restriction of their personal freedom.

All of the described changes in the lives of families undoubtedly influence their lifestyles. Lifestyle is a multidisciplinary topic that occurs in social sciences, economics and medicine. Originally, it was a sociological term introduced by Thorstein Vebler. Later, Max Weber linked lifestyle to economic situation, social structure and also consumption (Dworak 2009).

In sociological literature, the term lifestyle appeared in the 1970s and it has been understood in different ways until now. Other similar concepts, like everyday life, way of life, habits, ethos, etc., also lack precise, unambiguous meanings. In 1989, WHO defined lifestyle as a manner of being that results from a person's living conditions, their influence on the environment, individual behaviour patterns stemming from personality attributes and sociocultural factors. In behaviourist perspective, lifestyle is "a complex of repetitive behaviour patterns conditioned by control, living standard and economic possibilities of a given family or an individual" (Dworak 2009, 164).

In this scenario, lifestyle is a specific type of an individual's behaviour that manifests certain peculiarities and habits and that expresses human individuality: uniqueness. Thus, it is also one of the identifying signs of affiliation to a particular social stratum. Lifestyle also includes living standard, which is an expression of material conditions as means of satisfying basic human needs (Tokárová 2002).

In our research and throughout the present paper, lifestyle is understood as a complex of important actions, relations and connected practices that characterize a specific subject in everyday life (Duffková et al. 2007), i.e. the way people live, their living conditions, dietary habits, education, behaviour in different situations, entertainment, work, communication, actions, decisions, travels, beliefs and subscriptions to certain values, the way they bring up children, grow food, make products, etc. At the same time, lifestyle can be seen as an interdisciplinary issue that cannot be tackled and studied in its complexity from a single field's perspective.

Lifestyle includes:

- A complex (established structure) of activities by means of which people satisfy their needs;
- A complex of relations emerging in this cycle of life;
- A complex of values, norms and ideas (Pácl 1988).

As a complex of activities of a particular social group or an individual, which emphasizes their specific activities and values in individual stages of life, lifestyle is subject to frequent changes that result from acceptance of a different hierarchy of values, social position or autodidactic activity.

As a category, lifestyle is not only multidisciplinary, but also multidimensional. It is related to categories such as living standard, cultural level, values and value system or the currently very much discussed category of quality of life (Kraus et al. 2015).

The connection between lifestyle and quality of life is depicted in Fig. 1.1.

Our life takes place not just at a specific place, but also in a specific time. In this context, our lifestyle influences two spheres: occupational and non-occupational. From the lifestyle point of view, all non-occupational time includes an important area: leisure time. Because of that, this research and the whole present paper pay special attention to it.

The phenomenon of **leisure time** is of interest to a number of scientific disciplines; it is also becoming more and more urgent. This is primarily because of its increase and consequent growing role in everyone's life. It is no longer limited to the usual socializing function, as the compensatory (offsetting the strain of work or school), self-realizing and above all preventive (leisure time activities that allow

Fig. 1.1 Connection between lifestyle and quality of life (Blažej 2005)

using personal and value orientations as a part of protection from negative social phenomena and antisocial activities) functions become more important (Kraus 2008).

Health behaviour comprises a part of lifestyle that has a positive or negative impact on health. Health behaviour includes personal hygiene, body hygiene, physical activity, sleep, rest, diet, etc. It is also influenced by stress and the ability to eliminate it, use of intoxicating substances, aggression and violence, road traffic safety, control activities. Importantly, attitudes towards health are affected by upbringing and the process of socialization. Under the influence of various factors (behaviour examples, parental instructions, peers, school, mass media, religion, local community) that are mimicked and encountered in social interactions, a model emerges over childhood and adolescence, which can later be modified only with great difficulties.

Health was, is and beyond doubt will still be the highest value in human life. The notion of health is crucial for medicine; in the present, the following factors are considered determining and impactful (Machalová et al. 2009, p. 13).

Figure 1.2 shows clearly that while the role of genetic disposition and environment cannot be ignored and the quality of health care plays a certain role as well, lifestyle seems to be the deciding factor for an individual's medical condition.

Žumárová provides the following definition of **typical features of a lifestyle**:

Cognitive evaluation of oneself and one's own place in the world—a personal philosophy of life is the basic foundation of every individual's actions.

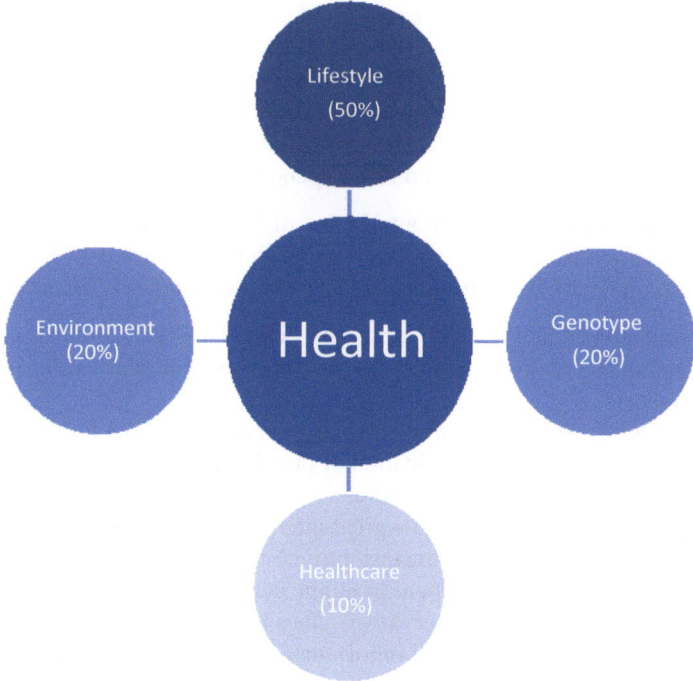

Fig. 1.2 Determinants of health

Manner of experiencing—the quality and intensity of experiences differ in individuals; the attempts to suppress natural emotions may even lead health problems.

Approach to work, relaxation and movement activity—one's mental capacities are most typically regenerated by compensatory self-realization; the ability to relax efficiently is a very important part of resting.

Coping with social interactions—for human beings, it is important to participate in a sufficient social network that provides them with a feeling of safety and on which they can rely; at the same time, however, one should not be too emotionally dependent on a single person, which leads to a loss of emotional autonomy.

Ego level—the overall personality endowment with the ability to handle difficult tasks in life (Žumárová 2001).

Lifestyles can be classified according to different criteria:

Havlík et al. (1996) divide lifestyles into the following three groups **according to prevailing values**:

- *Studying lifestyle* pertains to people who can be basically characterized by frequent reading and theatregoing, exploring trips, but also watching TV. For this group of people, curiosity is typical.

- *Lifestyle with play as the most common value* is a modified version of past cele-brations. Over the course of a year, every week and every day can be celebrated. This type of lifestyle is typical of athletes or sports fans as well as of players of various games and regular visitors of various entertainment venues.
- *Contemplative lifestyle* can occur both individually and in communities. Statistics show these are mostly loners who never spend their leisure time with families.

There are also other attempts at a typology of lifestyle. The German sociologist W. Georg perceives lifestyle as relatively stable, routine patterns of behaviour and action. Based on his findings, he construed the following types of lifestyle:

- *Hedonistic expressive lifestyle*—emphasis on social contacts and a network of friends and acquaintances; an individual rejects conventional family life as well as asceticism.
- *Family-oriented lifestyle*—family (also in the broader sense) forms the founda-tion of all aspects of life; prioritization of practical, useful hobbies; and minimal interest in politics, science and culture.
- *Culture-oriented ascetic lifestyle*—great interest in culture without emphasizing the significance of financial means; preference for healthy and eco-friendly lifestyle; and frequent engagement in public activities.
- *Careful passive lifestyle*—conservative values in various aspects of life; rejection of consumerism as well as anything avant-garde; avoidance of social contacts; and practically oriented.
- *Prestige-oriented self-presentation*—demonstration of social status in consump-tion as well as in leisure time; adherence to fashion trends; and extravagance.
- *Careful conventional lifestyle*—it differs from careful passive lifestyle by its emphasis on faith and religious values; conventional in terms of consumption and leisure time; and modesty and simplicity.
- *Avant-garde, pleasure-seeking and representative lifestyle*—consumption-focused; quality, exclusivity and extravagance are the leading principles; and emphasis on representative social contacts (Georg 1998).

The French sociologist **Bernard Cathelat** (1991) **created the following typology of lifestyle**:

- *Entrepreneur*—everything revolves around work; they frequently use modern products and means; in consumption, they prefer brands, originals, fashion; they are interested in current knowledge regarding any subject.
- *Utilitarian*—oriented towards family, home, traditions; their cultural interests are pragmatic, conservative, materialistic and regionalistic; and careful consumers.
- *Conservative*—enclosed within their own well-known "territory"; family-oriented; distrust of modern technologies; xenophobic but not fanatic patriots; and traditional approach to consumption as for the type of shop and the structure of purchase.
- *Ideal*—they desire a quiet family life, comfortable housing, abundance of leisure time; they are satisfied with themselves and have a very weak feeling of solidarity.

- *Anarchist*—preference for personal life; antisocial; pessimistic ironic observers; anticonsumerist views and preference for cultural underground; and not fond of books and cinema.
- *Opportunist–new rich*—"parasitic" lifestyle; preference for leisure time, holidays, narcissist sports; and they strive maximum personal gain without any regards for society.
- *Harlequin in the theatre of society*—they observe their existence, constantly reasserting their identity; fondness of videogames; preference for audio-visual and emotional information; and they like the fantastic and the shocking experiences.

Attempting to describe **lifestyle according to a set of everyday activities**, the following classification into several basic categories emerges:

Activities oriented towards job, profession and corresponding preparation—based on age, this covers the process of education, entering employment, adaptation to the work process, stabilization, professional growth–career, etc.

Activities related to family—they include search for a partner, starting a family, establishing and developing a household, upbringing of children, etc.

Activities related to interests—the delimitation of personal interests and their fostering and development together with a search for compromises necessitated by interests of other family members, rest, entertainment and relaxation.

Activities connected to social life—this means participating in social life and civic relations, expanding the area of social contacts and holding position in social and political life.

Activities connected to satisfaction of biological and hygienic needs—food, sleep, hygiene, etc. (Kraus 2008).

In relation to influencing individuals' lifestyles, **healthy lifestyle** has recently been discussed. It is a response to the condition of the Earth's population, especially in the developed countries, the information explosion, the influence of mass media as well as to the environmental situation and all negative aspects of scientific and technological developments, i.e. to the progress of civilization. Last but not least, as mentioned above, it is because of its crucial influence on human health.

Healthy lifestyle is not simply a matter of proper nutrition and sufficient movement; it is also related to mental health, which should be balanced, and an individual's social life. In the present, people tend to live in constant stress and rush and they are not able to relax adequately. We lack leisure time, and if we have some, we cannot use it properly.

Education towards healthy lifestyle is usually understood as instilling habits of body and mental hygiene. With regard to previously stated facts, **healthy lifestyle** is primarily related to these basic areas:

Rhythm of life—ratio of work and rest, physical and psychological strain, adequate length of sleep;

Movement regimen—regular physical activity and adequate physical strain;

Mental activity—connected to cultural interests and follow-up education that adheres to the principles of mental hygiene; and relaxation after everyday stress;

Regimen and rational nutrition—adequate dietary regimen that maintains health and both physical and mental performances;

Coping with difficult situations in life (Kraus 2008).

Lifestyle is formed by both objective and subjective factors. The subjective ones are relevant especially when considering an individual's lifestyle. Objective factors can be examined on different levels. First of all, there are the conditions and circumstances in the closest surroundings, which in this case mean family, but there can also be different microenvironments. Factors within local and regional surroundings can also have an impact. However, human lives are primarily determined by society-wide situations or even, in the globalized world of today, factors extending beyond the respective society.

There is another frequently discussed attribute of contemporary civilization: *consumer society*. It is not merely a negative feature; it is related to the development of technology and economy that led to elimination of hunger and destitution in the classical sense. Consumer society in a developed civilization presumes a certain economic standard of a mass consumer and in a way reflects an increased standard of living. A consumer needs to be able to buy consumer goods in order to be able to consume. Thus, it is necessary to re-evaluate a number of economic categories, especially wages and profit. Henry Ford can rightfully be considered the father of consumer society. For mass production of cars to be possible, there had to be consumers able to buy them. For this reason, he raised salaries. Mass production leads to an appropriate income and this causes mass consumption.

This is also related to *mass culture* and the vanishing or ailing traditional art, the so-called high culture. Art always produced and was supposed to produce delight; it is defined by its affective impact. Mass culture is dominated by a basic premise that it is created for the broadest strata of society: for the masses.

The contemporary society is also characterized by *increasing secularization of civilization*. This is manifested in a decreased influence of major religions with negative social impact (destabilization of morality and brute materialism). The place of major traditional religious systems is assumed by sectarian-type religions that lack the positive influence of large religions.

According to Fukuyma, all these serious issues (boundless individualism, huge societal dynamics including shifts in social norms and values, consumerist lifestyle, etc.) had the most profound impact on: (a) reproduction, (b) family, (c) relations between man and woman (Fukuyma 2006).

All of the described factors in family lifestyle, which includes a basic framework of activities and relations, have all of family members, in common. However, individual family members may invent their own style, which can differ in specific aspects (such as diet).

All of the aforementioned changes and transformations thoroughly influence family lifestyle, which is primarily affected by consumerism. In the present research, 20% of families gave shopping centre visits as a prevailing leisure time activity (Kraus and Jedličková 2007). This lifestyle also results in an already mentioned "monetization of childhood". Parents compensate for their inability to dedicate time to their own children by buying them anything the children ask for. However, this results in damage to children's personality development and may consequently lead to aberrant behaviour.

Lifestyle of contemporary families is also influenced by a shift in value orientation as material values are becoming more prominent than spiritual ones. This is also partially caused by a significant permeation of media into family life. Media have a profound impact on leisure time of individual family members and on their lifestyle overall.

Family lifestyle is in many ways related to the place of residence. The traditional division of urban and countryside environment has in the past decades also been subject to certain changes and shifts; however, it is expected some differences will endure.

Regarding the general perception of lifestyle of contemporary families, it seems to have become more differentiated. On the one hand, there is an increasing number of families that attempt to lead a healthy life, consider diet composition and try to be active in their leisure time, and on the other hand there continues to be a significantly larger group that does not embrace any principles of healthy diet, regimen or active life. As a result, the incidence of so-called lifestyle diseases rather tends to increase, especially among young people and children, and the populace's state of health worsens, let alone the impact of alcohol, tobacco products, drugs, violence, etc., on the youth's lives.

1.2 The Survey of Contemporary Family Lifestyle

1.2.1 Recent Research of Family

As a primary social group, primary educational institution and principal social institution, family is also a frequent subject of research and various surveys. Here, it has to be noted that methodologically, it is a highly complex issue for several reasons. Family is not only a primary social group, but also a group characterized by highly intimate relations. Thus, it is very difficult to penetrate this social institution's privacy, life and functioning. This research is likewise ethically sensitive. Moreover, the issue has recently become more complicated due to the universal emphasis on personal data privacy. For these reasons, research of family sometimes appears almost impossible. There are nevertheless numerous papers on family, including recent ones. Prior to describing the present survey Contemporary Family Lifestyle in Central European countries, this paper will take note of research done in the Czech Republic and Slovakia.

Some papers focus **on female and male role in family and on the division of labour**. In family and household, the "unequal" division of labour, responsibilities and rights according to gender is still produced and reproduced (Maříková 1999, 23). However, in contrast to the past, it tends to be emphasized that the lack of male participation in household labour (ironing, doing laundry, etc.) concerns both men and women. In males, there has been discovered a frequent unwillingness to take part in the so-called women's work, while in females, resignation has sometimes been found. In this context, it is remarkable that Holubová (2011) found that 33.5% of men want to participate more in domestic labour and 42.2% aim to be more active in childcare. In this respect, female expectations are always higher and more unequivocal (42.2% would prefer a greater participation in domestic work, and 76% want a greater activity in childcare).

According to Bútorová et al. (2008, 31–33), in the present there are relatively few people who openly proclaim the view that women should perform the majority of domestic labour and childcare. Such an opinion is only held by one-fifth of women (21%) and a little under one-third of men (29%). In comparison, 62% of women and 52% of men prefer cooperation of both spouses. Maříková's research (2006, 85) shows that mother continues to perform a very important role in family, since she is predominantly responsible for the most regular activities (i.e. everyday communication and basic care) and frequently also for the most time-consuming ones. Father participates alongside mother in such activities where regularity is less important (e.g. vocation-related decisions, punishment of children, buying presents).

Likewise, our research *Tradition and modernity in the life-style of the families of the Visegrad countries* shows a similar (or in some regions, even more unequal) situation regarding the division of responsibilities for the functioning of family and household; this research was performed in 2006 by universities in Katowice, Nitra, Hradec Králové and Szeged, where there was a coordinating centre (Kraus and Jedličková 2007). This is specifically illustrated in Table 1.1 (the figures show the percentage of participation of individual household members in specific tasks):

Clearly, there has been a shift in the traditional division of work in family; however, women remain more "competent" in domestic works than men. The fact that women play a significantly greater role in household maintenance than men has also been evidenced by Chaloupková (2005). Her research shows that on average, women spend twice as much time on household chores as men (23.5 h and 11 h 42 min, respectively) and perform the majority of domestic activities. Women always or mostly take care of washing and ironing clothes (94% of women sharing a household with a partner), cooking (80%), tidying up (73%) and washing dishes (72%). The model where men and women share these responsibilities occurs in a third of the cases at most. There are rare households in which these activities are performed by men; their number, however, has been increasing recently.

A number of studies are focused **on public perception of family, marriage, loose partnership and parenthood**. An interesting comparison on this issue has been provided by the paper *Attitudes towards marriage, parenthood and family roles in the Czech Republic and in Europe* by Chaloupková and Šalamounová (2004), which employed the data analysis of the ISSP research. Within the ISSP programme, two surveys called family and gender roles took place in 1994 and 2002 in the Czech Republic. The Czech set of data within ISSP 2002 provided information on 1289

Table 1.1 Participation of individual household members in specific tasks (in %)

Activity	Father	Mother	Child	Grandparents	Everyone
1. Shopping	16.7	64.5	1.7	8.8	7.8
2. Tidying up	6.9	81.3	4.0	4.2	9.0
3. Cooking	6.2	82.7	0.4	4.6	2.9
4. Washing clothes	3.8	86.7	1.3	4.2	1.0
5. Ironing	3.3	85.4	3.1	3.5	1.0
6. Accompanying children from/to kindergarten/school	6.7	23.3	1.2	4.2	2.1
7. Paying bills	45.9	41.5	0.3	6.3	3.7
8. Handling official matters	43.9	40.8	0.6	8.5	4.8
9. Gardening	18.6	29.8	0.6	5.4	1.3
10. Lawn mowing	41.2	9.2	3.1	3.5	1.8
11. Pet care	10.6	16.8	7.9	2.9	6.8
12. Small repairs in the house	71.8	13.1	2.7	3.3	1.9
13. Dishwashing	11.7	61.8	6.0	6.3	7.5
14. Helping children with homework	8.8	30.6	0.2	3.7	1.9
15. Playing/walking with children	8.7	32.9	0.6	7.9	3.1
16. Taking out garbage	25.6	31.0	24.8	6.9	9.6

respondents. The data was gathered by means of a multidegree random selection. In 1994, the data was collected from 1024 respondents by the universities' agency.

Both surveys used a set of seven questions regarding attitudes towards marriage and other types of family organization. Furthermore, the survey contained two questions specifically focused on the value of children in individual life. The following statements were included:

- In general, married men and women are happier than single ones.
- Bad marriage is better than no marriage.
- People who want to have children should enter into marriage.
- A single parent can provide as adequate an upbringing to a child as two parents working together.
- It is perfectly fine when people live together without planning marriage.
- It is beneficial when people who want to enter a marriage live together for some time.
- Usually, divorce is the best solution of a situation in which a couple are no longer able to resolve their marital issues.
- Watching children grow is the greatest joy in life.
- People who have never had children are leading an empty life.

Among respondents, the greatest number agreed with the statement that watching children grow is the greatest joy in life. In comparison with the 1990s, the support even grew, up to 90%. More than a half of participants also thought that people who have never had children are leading an empty life. In this case, there was a 10% increase in comparison with 1994. On the other hand, the view of cohabitation of two unmarried partners has not changed significantly. Almost three-thirds of respondents thought people should first try out living together and only then enter into marriage. For a half of the respondents, it was acceptable that partners live together without planning a marriage. This statement unfortunately does not show the extent to which people accept these types of relationships in case a child is born to the couple. Two questions focused on family organization after a family welcomes a child. Forty percentage thought one parent can provide as good an upbringing as two parents working together. In comparison with the previous survey, the share grew by 14%. There was a similar decrease in the support for the statement that people who want to have children should enter a marriage (almost 60% in 2002). Forty-two percentage of respondents thought people are generally happier in marriage, meaning there was almost no change in contrast to 1994.

There has also been no change in attitudes towards divorce. Sixty percentage of respondents viewed it as the best solution of marital problems. The least supported statement was that bad marriage is better than no marriage. However, in 2002 the statement was supported by 10% more people than at the beginning of the 1990s (16%).

In relation to education, age and a number of children, results from 1994 did not differ significantly from the findings from 2002 stated above.

The results are remarkable in comparison with Slovakia, Poland, Hungary, Sweden, Netherlands, France and Spain. Individual countries showed relatively large differences in the degree of support for individual statements. As expected, the protestant countries Sweden and Netherlands proved the most tolerant for alternative family structures. The respondents from these two countries perceived unmarried partnership as an equal alternative to marriage more frequently (90%). In the least cases of all countries, they associated childbirth with a need to enter marriage (less than a third). In more cases, they also disagreed with the claim that childless people lead an empty life (one in ten only). Among Dutch respondents, there was a relatively lesser support for the statement that it is beneficial when people who want to enter a marriage live together for some time. However, this in fact might have evidenced their tolerance; the respondents could have felt it is each couple's responsibility, which was why they did not agree with the wording.

Respondents from all former socialist countries more frequently felt that people are happier in marriage: a half of them agreed with the statement, with Slovakia showing a little lesser support. In countries that have been in the EU longer, only every fourth person (at most) agreed with the statement. The respondents from post-communist countries also showed the least support for both statements regarding unmarried partners.

The statements that one parent can provide as good an upbringing as two garnered a surprisingly high support in Poland and Spain. Both these countries are highly Catholic in comparison with the rest. The reason for such a widespread opinion might have been, to an extent, the negative perception of abortion; the respondents might have felt it was better if a child was born even in an incomplete family. In the

Czech Republic, there was a comparatively high support in 2002 for the statement that bad marriage is better than no marriage; almost one in five agreed. In other countries, it was one in ten at most (Spain and Poland) and two out of a hundred (Netherlands).

With the exception of Netherlands, the most supported statement was that watching children grow is the greatest joy in life. Hungary showed the greatest rate of support (95%); however, the differences from the Czech Republic and other countries were minimal. In Netherlands, only eight in ten people supported this statement.

For some statements, the influence of gender was marked. In all states, women showed a statistically significant increase in the view that one parent can provide as good an upbringing as both parents. In case of partners split, women take care of children almost exclusively. Because of this, most women felt only one parent can also cope with the situation. In most countries, men thought married people are happier than singles (except for Slovakia). In France, Netherlands and Sweden, men stated more frequently that people who plan to have children should enter into marriage. In these countries, the experience with informal partnerships has been more extensive; thus, men may have felt the disadvantages of these types of cohabitation, especially in cases when a couple with children split.

The influence of education on individual answers was lesser among Slovaks and the Dutch. In all countries, less educated people were more conservative (including the abovementioned ones); however, they usually agreed with the statement regarding divorce. On the other, people, graduates of secondary schools with a final examination and universities tended to agree with the statements concerning unmarried couples and did not feel people should enter marriage because of children (Chaloupková and Šalamounová 2004).

The research performed by the Institute of Sociology of the Czech Academy of Sciences that was focused on the relations between changes in job market and in private life examined the extent to which family lifestyle is influenced by **the time dedicated to work** (Dudová 2005). This survey took place in the last quarter of 2005 and included 5510 respondents aged 25–54 let (2778 males and 2732 females) selected via the method of quota sampling.

This representative survey also focused on the influence of marital status on time dedicated to work, showing that in females, time demands of work had no relation to marital status as the distribution was identical in all categories. It is therefore not possible to claim that married women work less intensely in their salaried jobs than single and divorced women.

However, in males, time demands of work were clearly dependent on marital status. Divorced men spent most time working, and married ones most frequently worked with an average intensity. Unexpectedly, single males did not work more intensely than others; in fact, this category included the greatest number of respondents who worked less intensely or not at all. This corresponds to the fact that single males are members of lower social and economic classes and include higher share of economically inactive individuals than other categories of marital status.

Respondents' marital status also influenced their willingness to work at weekends. A decidedly highest rate was found among divorced males without a stable partner

(60%). Among women, however, this was not the case, probably because they had to take care of children from previous marriages.

The extensive research of family life in Slovakia in the context of social transformation was performed by the UMB in Banská Bystrica (Višňovský et al. 2010).

It focused on demographic development and an increase in divorce rate, family behaviour, unemployment and its impact on family life, troubles in family functions, stress situations in family and relevant coping strategies, occurrence of sociopath logical phenomena in families, surrogate family care and cooperation of family and school, with a special attention paid to Roma families.

P. Ondrejkovič performed a remarkable survey focused on the influence of current social conditions, which include rapid change, on family life, entitled *The Manifestation of Anomie in Contemporary Slovak Family* (Ondrejkovič 2010). He noted that contemporary "modern" family is inconsistent, its internal relations are chaotic, its structure changes frequently, and it often produces feelings of helplessness. In a growing number of cohabitations, helplessness was typical, together with a difficult grasp of the contemporary complex world, which lacks clear rules and standards; this produced feelings of loneliness, pessimistic moods, indifference and apathy.

Notably, results and conclusions of this survey showed that out of all questions, the highest score was achieved by the answers "As an individual, I cannot change anything about our current troubles" and "The world has become so complex today one can no longer grasp it". Overall, the author claimed that the symptoms of anomie in contemporary family were proved beyond doubt (Ondrejkovič 2010).

The already mentioned survey *Tradition and modernity in the life-style of the families of the Visegrad countries* (Kraus and Jedličková 2007) was focused directly at **family lifestyle**. Given the general trends in recent family transformations, it is possible to supplement this by a demonstration of the extent to which there has been a shift away from tradition towards modern lifestyle, beginning with cultural habits. Table 1.2 shows that family life has been most affected in the Czech Republic and Hungary. On the contrary, Polish and Slovak families have been keeping traditional habits and customs to a significantly greater degree, and they are more conservative.

The situation is similar regarding value orientation (Table 1.3). In this case, modernization has most influenced the value system of families in the Czech Republic and also in Hungary. The greatest adherence to traditional values has been discovered in Poland.

Table 1.2 Family cultural habits in terms of subjective indicators (as % of the national sample)

Cultural habits of the family subjective	Hungary $n = 458$	Poland $n = 492$	Czech Republic $n = 520$	Slovakia $n = 494$	Total $N = 1964$
Traditional	65.9	75.2	64.4	75.7	70.3
Modern	34.1	24.8	35.6	24.3	29.7
Total	100	100	100	100	100

Table 1.3 Family value system in terms of subjective indicators (as % of the national sample)

Value system subjective	Hungary $n = 454$	Poland $n = 473$	Czech Republic $n = 515$	Slovakia $n = 494$	Total $N = 1936$
Traditional	71.6	81.0	68.9	76.5	74.4
Modern	28.4	19.0	31.1	23.5	25.6
Total	100	100	100	100	100

The following part of this chapter is dedicated to methodological basis of the present survey.

1.2.2   The Research Project Contemporary Family Lifestyle

Aims of the Research

The aim of this research was to ascertain the lifestyle of contemporary families. It was performed, as noted in the introduction, in the project "Development and Support of the Multidisciplinary Scientific and Research Team for the Study of Contemporary Family at the UHK", which included the topic "Contemporary Family Lifestyle".

The research team established the following partial aims in four areas:

- Life satisfaction:

  - How respondents picture a happy family.
  - What influences the happiness of a family.

- Economic situation of families:

  - What the main income is and who contributes to it.
  - What the biggest costs are associated with.
  - How much the families have been influenced by unemployment and dependence on social welfare.
  - How they perceive their living standard.

- Family spare time:

  - What the proportion is of time spent on one's own to time spent together.
  - How much spare time individual family members have.
  - What activities constitute spare time occupation.
  - Whether family spent their spare time according to their wishes.

- Media in the family:

  - Equipment of households by selected types of electronic media.
  - Frequency and manner of using media in the family.
  - Attitudes towards the role of media in family life.

The stated entries will also be examined for a connection to independent variables: the size of the place of residence, the number of children in the family, parents' age, job, attained education.

1.2.3 Method Employed

The issue of examining lifestyle is highly problematic. It has to be noted that lifestyle is such a multifarious category and it is virtually almost unrecordable empirically. It is linked to a number of other categories that are also difficult to grasp, such as the tempo of life, the rhythm of life, the intensity of life, life orientation, self-experiencing, the meaning of life, life ideals and the harmony of life (Petrusek et al. 1996).

Despite these caveats and difficulties, lifestyle is researched, or at least some of its components are. That is also the case here; the aforementioned categories of lifestyle were selected. Lifestyle can then be examined from the perspective of lifecycle stages, generational perspective, territorial perspective, etc. These variables were also considered in the present research.

There are various techniques available to gain specific data, e.g. a time-lapse photography in relation to examining spare time. Quantitative research performed via anonymous questionnaire in the family was selected to the empirical inquiry.

A custom non-standardized questionnaire (see Appendix) was chosen as the most suitable research technique. When preparing the questionnaire, there were selected fields which functioned as a basis—satisfaction with life, economic situation of families, family spare time and media in the family. Its advantage was a relatively quick and economic collection of a relatively large amount of data from a corresponding number of respondents. The disadvantage was that it was only possible to discover the perception the respondents had of themselves, i.e. their subjective perspective of reality, not their real nature. Thus, the data may be slightly distorted.

During the preparation of the questionnaire, the effectiveness of each item and the appositeness of its formulation were evaluated, with a special attention paid to the assessment of the relevance of items for the research aims. The questionnaire contained 31 questions/items. The questions had the form of closed items, closed polychromous items, half-closed items and open items. The first five questions inquired about sociodemographic data (the place of residence, the number of children in the family, age, attained education and employment of both spouses/partners). The remaining questioned were intended to provide data for the remaining four areas: 6–11 economic situation of families; 12–14 happiness and living standard of families; 15–22 and 30 spare time in the family; and 23–29 media in the family. Thus, besides inquiring about the abovementioned independent variables (the place of residence, age, etc.), the questionnaire also included questions ascertaining what the family income was, who the earner was, whether the family received any welfare or whether family members had any experience of unemployment, what the greatest costs in family budget were associated with and whether the family manage to save some money.

Further items were focused on what amount and quality of spare time were available, which spare time activities were the most typical of the family, which activities the family members would have liked to do and why it was not possible, whether they engaged in sports, how often and in what types of sports, and whether they played video games.

The research also enquired which media were available in the household, who used them most often and how frequently it was, whether family members watched TV together and what type of shows they preferred, and how the media influenced the family life (question no. 26).

The category of satisfaction with life was also covered. Despite marked differences, most definitions of life satisfaction, happiness and subjective well-being share the emphasis on the subjectivity of the assessment—people are satisfied if they feel that way or if they state they feel that way—people are happy and content, if they say they are. Can happiness and satisfaction be measured?

At the same time, the issues inherent in a survey of satisfaction with life, happiness and subjective well-being are not limited to the rather small consensus on what the terms really mean. Empirical sociology also raises the question whether and how happiness or satisfaction can be measured. For this purpose, psychologists created complex indices; however, life satisfaction/happiness is generally measured in a few questions or even in a single question asking respondents how happy/satisfied they are.

Using more questions and scales is certainly better than only using a single one; surprisingly, however, both methods of measurement have the same reliability. Even it seems a crude research tool at first glance, the results of discussions and long-term research show that even a simple question (or questions) may meaningfully record individual satisfaction, which can then be considered in the context of demographic and social factors (Hamplová 2004, 13). The present research employed this procedure and included questions regarding how the respondents imagine a happy family, what they would need to be satisfied and which aspect of life has the greatest impact on life satisfaction.

1.2.4 Research Sample and the Course of the Survey

The questionnaires were distributed by students of both daily and combined study programmes at the Faculty of Education of the UHK. Given that the students did not come from Eastern Bohemia only, the research sample covered a majority of the country and could be considered relatively representative, given the overall number of 1307 questionnaires. The questionnaires were transmitted to families; family was understood as a cohabitation of at least one parent and one supported child (i.e. a child from birth to graduation, including university graduation, living in one household).

Parents were defined as both partners in an informal relationship and married couples. The survey aimed at an even distribution, including parents according to the size of the place of residence and according to their education. Thus, the respondents primarily included parents, who provided answers to the questions in the survey for whole families.

The survey took a similar form in other countries, specifically in Slovakia, Poland, Germany, Ukraine and Latvia. The questionnaires were also distributed by students of collaborating universities. Even though the research samples in these countries were not even, we believe it is possible to perform a comparison.

The numbers of respondents were as follows: Czech Republic: 1307 respondents, Slovakia: 288 respondents, Poland: 126 respondents, Ukraine: 209 respondents, Latvia: 381 respondents and Germany: 126 respondents.

The collection of data took place from May to October 2013. In foreign countries, the process was more difficult and continued until the end of 2014. The data in questionnaires was processed gradually, and incomplete or faulty questionnaires were excluded. The gathered data was recorded (encoded) into a prepared template in MS Excel and subsequently exported to the statistics software SPSS. There, the data was checked and divided into nominal, ordinal and metrical for the purposes of further processing. Nominal data was further categorized into the most frequent types (e.g. for items nos. 8, 11, 13, 16, 28 of the questionnaire).

Selected figures concerning research samples:

The respondents' spread of age in all included countries was 25–65 in males and 20–55 in females. The majority of respondents were aged 25–45.

Regarding the number of children in families, in all countries except for Germany and Slovakia, three quarters of families had one or two children. In both Germany and Slovakia, they only comprised a little over a half of the total number. The German research sample was set apart by the number of childless families (25.4%). In Slovakia, on the other hand, 30.6% of families had three children, while the share of such families in all other countries was roughly 10%.

In terms of attained education, the research sample of males comprised virtually in all included countries roughly two-thirds of secondary school graduates, with the exception of Germany (just under 40%). Roughly one in four graduated from university (only 14% in Slovakia and 33% in Germany). The representation of respondents who attained basic education was minimal (highest in Latvia—6%).

The spread was similar in females, but university education was less frequent (especially in Latvia—16%, and in Slovakia and Poland—19%). The share of respondents who attained basic education was also neglectable.

References

Beck, U. (1986). *Risikogeselschaft. Auf dem Weg in eine andere Moderne.* Frankfurt am Main: Suhrkamp Verlag.

Blažej, A. (2005). Kvalita života z aspektu udržatělného rozvoja v 21. storočí. In *Kvalita života a rovnosťpríležitostí. Acta facultatis philosophicae universitatis Prešoviensis Humanistický sborník 10.* Prešov: FF PU.

Bútorová, Z., a kol. (2008). *Ona a on na Slovensku. Zaostrené na rod a vek.* Bratislava: IVO.

Cathelat, B. (1991). *Panorama des styles de vie 1960–1990.* Paris: Les Editions d'organisation.

Chaloupková, J. (2005). Faktory ovlivňující dělbu domácí práce v českých domácnostech a hodnocení její spravedlnosti. *Sociologickj5 časopis/Czech Sociological Review,* (41), 57–77.

Chaloupková, J., & Šalamounová, P. (2004). *Postoje k manželství, rodičovství a k rolím v rodině v ČR a v Evropě.* Praha: SÚ AV ČR.

Dudová, R. (2005). *Rodina a rodiny – formy soukromého života v ČR.* Praha: Sociologický ústav AV ČR.

Duffková, J., Urban, L., & Dubský, J. (2007). *Sociologie životního stylu.* Praha: Policejní akademie.

Dworak, A. (2009). Rodina a životní styl – perspektiva sociální pedagogiky. In *Sociální pedagogika ve střední Evropě – současnj5 stav a perspektivy. Sborník z mezinárodní konference* (pp. 122–128). Brno: IMS.

Fukuyma, F. (2006). *Velký rozvrat.* Praha: Academia.

Georg, W. (1998). *Soziale Lage und Lebensstil: eine Typologie.* Opladen: Leske + Budrich.

Hamplová, D. (2004). *Životní spokojenost: rodina, práce a další faktory.* Praha: Portál.

Havlík, R., Halászová, J. M., & Prokop, J. (1996). *Kapitoly ze sociologie výchovy.* Praha: PdF KU.

Holubová, B. (2011). *Súhrnná správa o stave rodovej rovnosti na Slovensku rok 2010.* Bratislava: Inštitút pre výskum rodiny.

Kraus, B. (2008). *Základy sociální pedagogiky.* Praha: Portál.

Kraus, B., & Jedličková, I. (2007). National report from the Czech Republic, University of HradecKrálové. In Z. Benkö (Ed.), *Tradition and modernity in the life-style of the families of the Visegrad countries.* Szeged: SZEK J. Gyula Higher Education Publisher.

Kraus, B., et al. (2015). *Životní styl současné české rodiny.* Hradec Králové: Gaudeamus.

Machalová, J., Kubátová, D., et al. (2009). *Výchova ke zdraví.* Praha: Grada Publishing.

Maříková, H. (1999). *Muž v rodině: demokratizace sféry soukromé.* Praha: SÚ AV ČR.

Maříková, H. (2006). Genderový aspekt rodičovství. In D. Hamplová, et al. (Eds.), *Životní cyklus sociologické a demografické perspektivy.* Praha: Sociologický ústav AV ČR.

Ondrejkovič, P. (2010). *Prejavy anómie v súčasnej slovenskej rodine.* Nitra: UKF.

Pácl, P. (1988). *Sociologie životního způsobu.* Praha: SPN.

Petrusek, M., a kol. (1996). *Velký sociologický slovník.* Praha: Karolinum.

Schneewind, K. (1998). *Wandel der Familie. Hofrege.* Bern: Göttingen.

Sullerot, E. (1998). *Krize rodiny.* Praha: Karolinum.

Tokárová, A. (2002). K metodologickým otázkám výskumu a hodnotenia kvality života. In *Kvalita života v kontextoch globalizácie a vj5konovej spoločnosti. Acta facultatis philosophicae universitatis Prešoviensis.* Prešov: FF PU.

Višňovský, L., Hroncová, J., et al. (2010). *Slovenská rodina v kontexte transformačnj5ch premien.* Banská Bystrica: UMB.

Žumárová, M. (2001). Životní styl a jeho utváření. In B. Kraus, V. Poláčková, et al. (Eds.), *Člověk, prostředí, výchova.* Brno: Paido.

Chapter 2
Characteristics of Family Lives in Central Europe

Abstract In this chapter, authors give a picture of families in individual countries, which participated in the survey, so from the Czech Republic, Slovakia, Germany, Poland, Ukraine and Latvia. They pay attention mainly to the family changes after the year 1990. There is mainly demographic situation. Furthermore, there are features which present contemporary family such as an increase of democratization in family coexistence in connection with the shifts of roles and disintegration in a family life linked with overall individualism manifested by automation, where one creates his/her own way of life. The contemporary family is more likely affected in all countries by progressive social differentiation; in a different level of unemployment, certain isolation and changes are always seen in intergeneration relationships. The authors also pay attention to family social policy and housing situation when starting a family.

Keywords Family · Demographic situation · Form of coexistence · Democratization · Socioeconomic situation · Disintegration · Isolation · Generational problems · Culture

2.1 The Image of the Czech Family

The change of a sociopolitical situation after the year 1990 has brought impacts into not only the economic sphere but also cultural and social sphere which has affected also a family life. Czech society is coming back among modern societies, as it was pulled out from its place for almost a half of a century. But it also returns to the core of capitalism. During its return, where it had already been it finds a different capitalism, not the one that was created as ground plan a half a century ago.

If we are successful, we have perspective and wealth. How does this system support family? The *development of the number of new flats* is considered to be the most significant for post-revolution history.

The housing crisis was not improved by the new regime, but it even was made more difficult. The fact, that almost more than one-third of the population aged 25–29 years, undoubtedly adults, does not have their own flat, would have seemed

© The Author(s) 2020
B. Kraus et al., *Contemporary Family Lifestyles in Central and Western Europe*,
SpringerBriefs in Sociology, https://doi.org/10.1007/978-3-030-48299-2_2

unsustainable in an industrially advanced society. Nevertheless, it did not rank among the highest priorities of a social transformation.

There were set certain rules up to 1990 (duty to be employed, parents were responsible for their child to attend school). Suddenly *unemployment is rising* that affects the family stability and demographic situation and also has indirect impact on family breakdown. There is a gradual diversion from traditions in terms of there are more women who want to become mothers but not to be married, or even not to live with a partner. Establishing a family becomes a dilemma mainly for young women.

The basic issue in the lives of families is "to have time for a family" and ability to utilize it. Family life should be enriching but nowadays is more likely "exhausting". We talk about so-called sandwich generation. On the one hand, there are worries about children, and on the other hand there are worries about parents.

Traditional social standards of family behaviour create conflict with individual aspirations of young people. This fact may have consequences that cannot be simply assessed as positive or negative. Exemption from these traditional standards allows us to succeed in more demanding conditions of market-oriented, dynamic and open society (and it is obviously perceived that way); however, increasing individualism weakens family bonds and aspiration.

Contemporary family remains monogamous, but it is a kind of *serial monogamy, where* an individual changes several partners during his/her lifetime. At the same time, the relation has more character of a partnership than a marriage. This is partly due to secularization of the family. The family bond which should have lasted forever has ceased.

In addition to that, another live model, "single", is being extended. An increasing number of young people perceive family as restriction of personal freedom. One-third of the households in our society consist of the live model "single". The phenomenon of singles is perceived by us as well as in the world as new, and it disturbs social policy. Single people represent threat, because they bring lack of solidarity and insensitivity towards the concept of sustainable development according to the fact that they do not have children (Tomášek 2006). If we had respected traditional family definition (baptism and marriage), then more and more cohabitation could not have been considered as a family.

The classic family becomes to be just one of the alternatives. This is not just about the economic crisis, but about the fundamental cultural change. At the same time, this process is sometimes adaptive to the way of family life, other times it is destructive and it threatens family values. Family forms and functions are being changed in the changing world because a family is living, constantly evolving social institution. This creates *alternative forms of family cohabitation*, which are conditioned by their change of society status.

These are the following:

1. Free coexistence (cohabitation);
2. Multiple (series of) relationships (life patterns of successive relationships);
3. Separated families and in divorce proceedings;
4. Single-parent families (death, divorce, birth outside marriage);

5. Binuclear families (divorced, separated couple, where the second biological parent is interested, mutual responsibility for the child even in different households);
6. Repeated marriages;
7. Stepfamilies (at least one parent has a child from a previous relationship);
8. Homosexual, lesbian families (a child from former heterosexual relationship, adopted child) (Kučírek 2014).

What are the characteristic attributes of Czech family in recent years?

There are new aspects of **demographic development**, such as natural population decline and increasing population ageing. Another significant shift occurred in marriage age. In men, the figure has increased from age 24 to 29, and in women from 21 to 24. There has been a substantial decrease of birth rate. While in the beginning of the 1990s, the coefficient amounted to 1.9, in recent years it has been roughly 1.4.

This has been influenced by economic problems, unemployment and housing situation. Today, a child in a family is very often perceived (by both parents) as a barrier to professional development or an obstacle of self-realization.

However, a child is often also perceived as a certain luxury because of economic reasons. The results of J. Macháčková's research manifest clearly that in relation to an arrival of a child, the change of both social and economic situations of a family occurs, parents expect greater difficulties in return to employment and overall, and a child's arrival creates a problem for families. The author states that the conditions that arise when starting a new family are not particularly favourable; the Czech state institutions do not seem to heed this unsatisfactory state (Macháčková 2008). It is not surprising that there is a significant increase in the number of marriages, in which only one child is considered, while some young people do not plan to have a child at all.

Another shift in the nature of family is significant. Because of the decrease of lawfully established families, there is a rising trend of unmarried cohabitation. In the 1970s, 95% of children were born in marriages. In the present, however, the percentage of children born outside of wedlock reaches almost 50% (see the following chart).

One of the phenomena occurring relatively frequently in the present day is divorce of parents. Divorce or break-up of cohabitation is frequently present in views of the youth of today as a "safeguard" of a potential failure. Divorce itself is stressful for parents and, even more so, for children. As Matějček and Dytrych (1997) argue, it is necessary to realize that children are exposed to psychological strain, the consequences of which may often not show immediately afterwards or may not be recognized in time. The consequence of the strain can be manifested, e.g. in behavioural patterns as late as in pubescence or at the beginning of adolescence.

Divorce is frequently perceived as beneficial for relations and atmosphere and as a way to peace. It has been demonstrated, however, that in most marriages, the stressful atmosphere filled with tension and arguments remains. In an overwhelming majority of cases, parents live separately after the divorce. Problems of where and when the child will live appear.

The **democratization of family** life in recent decades occurred primarily as a result of long-term efforts of women for emancipation in all aspects of life. At the same time, it is related to an increasing level of education and qualification of women and to a certain degree also to transformations of value orientation. Moreover, there are shifts in roles, especially a decline of male and father authority. Some authors even consider this a crisis of fatherhood. That can also be manifested mainly in relation to personality development and upbringing of boys as a problem that contributes to deviant behaviour.

The tendency towards democratization is notable not only between spouses but also in the child–parent relations. It was not so long ago when children addressed their parents in a formally polite way. Overall, relations in the present tend towards a part-nership and also to a much more tolerant approach to children. It is again debatable whether this transformation is unambiguously beneficial for personality development of children and whether this "friendship" is not abused by children, which is mani-fested in a complete lack of recognition of authority, which consequently contributes to elimination of any restraints in behaviour.

The existence of family is essential for **economic growth**, as it contributes signif-icantly to what has recently been called "human capital". Family has also functioned (and frequently, continues to do so in the present) as a separate economic unit that takes part in production of social wealth. Under the influence of the aforementioned dangers of today, especially in relation to a continuing differentiation of society, differentiation of families also occurs and their socio-economic situation changes. Overall, since the 1990s, a certain decrease in actual income and a concentration of the majority of households in lower-income classes have become evident.

In this research (realized in the group of 500 families within the Tradition and modernity in the life-style of the families of the Visegrad countries project), a half of the families stated debts and in almost 60% of cases indicated that price is essential when they are shopping for food (Kraus and Jedličková 2007, p. 279). On the other hand, there are numerous families that live in excessive abundance; in these cases, the so-called monetization of childhood in the form of disproportionately high allowance occurs frequently.

In the present, the lifestyle of many families is determined by their socio-economic situation, which sometimes becomes a direct risk factor for all the members, especially children. Both extremes are dangerous.

For some time now, it has been noticeable that **disintegration of family life** has grown. In almost all families, time spent together by sharing experiences, joys and worries, and looking for mutual help and cooperation has diminished. On the contrary, there are increasing numbers of families in which their members only meet and exchange messages, or stop communicating entirely. For instance, to a large degree, families do not even meet over meals. In case of dinner, 43% reported meeting daily and 15% at weekends only, while in case of lunch, 45% meet at weekends (Kraus and Jedličková 2007). In a way, family has become a space of passage in which its members live next to each other rather than together.

The matter of communication is absolutely essential for a functioning family. The present surveys also confirm that family ties are strengthened by factors such as mutual communication, shared interests and leisure time spent together. Only then, e.g. eroticism or sexuality follows. In this survey, the most frequent response (88%) to the question about what keeps a family together the most was: "I can rely on someone, I have emotional support" (Kraus and Jedličková 2007, p. 298).

Contemporary family also seems to be more closed off, which leads to certain **isolation**; the lives of their members are directed inwards. In this way, family is growing smaller not only as far as numbers of members are concerned, but also in terms of the number and intensity of mutual attachments. It is therefore overall more unstable and sensitive to any inner turmoil. Because of non-existing external anchoring to broader social bonds, any conflicts or other problems figuratively throw family off balance, and situations can very quickly develop into conditions that endanger the whole stability and may even lead to a collapse (Kraus 2008). The phenomenon of isolation is also related to the fact there has been a substantial increase in the number of single-person households. This pertains not only to the model of life as a "single", but also to seniors who live alone and people who were abandoned and did not choose this way of life. According to statistics, out of 4,366,218 households in the Czech Republic almost a third consist of only one person. This trend is growing; therefore, it is assumed that by 2030, single-person households will comprise more than 35% of the total number.

As a consequence of profound changes in the situation both within families and in the society, **intergenerational relations** also transform, which is accompanied by many issues. Given increasing life expectancy, there is a coexistence of three or even four generations. Currently, there are 80,000 elderly citizens who depend on the support of others (usually within their families); it is expected that in 2030, this number will increase to 150,000. Apparently, for 20% of families who provide care, such situation is very difficult, especially financially. Intergenerational relations are also affected by increased retirement age and job market situation (e.g. there has been a decrease in availability of grandmothers in pre-retirement age).

However, it has been proved that grandparents have an important influence on children and help fulfil socializing and educational functions of family (different values, models, etc.).

In today's society (especially among the youth), it is often declared "this is no age for old people". Displays of ageism are becoming more frequent, and the elderly are subjected to domestic violence. Ageism is manifested in the emphasis on a cult of youth and in disparagement of old age. The key factors of ageism are the stereotypes regarding old age which are commonly accepted by the society.

It is typical of Czech families that only a small fraction of the elderly share a household with their children (6%), while most of them live relatively close by, in the same town or even village (Vágnerová 2007).

The present research reached the following conclusions. The way of maintaining contacts between adult children and their parent (grandparents) was following: at least several times a week—phone calls in 30% of cases and visits: roughly 9%; several times a month—phone calls: 11% and personal visits: 24%. Grandparents help espe-cially with childcare (28%), financially (20%), materially (25%) and with various works (10%). Parents help grandparents above all with household maintenance (28%) and by providing care (18%) (Kraus and Jedličková 2007, p. 299).

According to E. Mendelová, contemporary family can be characterized by the following attributes:

Nuclear family is losing its ritualized form. Legalization of cohabitation of partners is currently no longer necessary for family life, and a growing number of families are based on cohabitation of unmarried partners.

Discontinuity of generations and transformation of family structure. There is a decrease not only in the number of children in the family, but also in intergenerational cohabitation, while the number of single-person households grows.

Decrease in stability of family. In the past decades, there has been an increase in divorce rate due to both objective (process of emancipation and growth of atheism) and subjective reasons (marriage is based on emotional basis).

Changes in organization of family cycle. People become parents at an older age, and children are born only after certain duration of marriage or cohabitation of partners. People who become grandparents tend to be older but often still working.

Dual-career marriages. Due to increasing levels of education and qualification, and consequently also of an employment rate of women, the time parents spend with their children and other family members decreases.

Increasing life expectancy means families exist longer after the children leave. Children also live in a shared household with their parents for a longer time.

Greater emphasis on material values. There is an obvious effort to reach a living standard equal to other developed countries and secure greater convenience, privacy and affluence (Mendelová 2014, pp. 13–14).

In conclusion, it is possible to add that despite all manifestations of a certain crisis of family, it has paradoxically in a way become more important as a refuge from the complex public world of the present day and poses, especially within socially weak contexts, as the only space of support for its members, especially children. Following J. Macháčková, it is possible to state that in spite of all changes that family has gone and continues to go through, it remains the best environment for healthy development of children (Macháčková 2008).

2.2 The Image of the German Family

In August 2017, the Minister of Family Affairs, Katharina Barley, presented the German family report 2017 with the following main results: the number of unmarried couples and the number of births (also from academics) increase, but even the number of poor families (also migrants) with minor education and minor chances to develop increases. The percentage of divorces decreases, and there is more acceptance of the diversity of modern families (Bundesministerium für Familie, Senioren, Frauen und Jugend 2017).

In July 2017, a change of the marriage law now offers everybody to get married—independent from sex and sexual orientation.

How do families feel nowadays? Which models (concepts) help to stand the conflict between traditional institution of marriage and individually created way of life—between tradition and change? And what about the children? This chapter takes a look on modern families in Germany, their issues, their specific problems and consequences for children and their education. The data is taken from up-to-date studies: AOK Familienstudie 2014 a research of Sinus Institutes; the Children Media Study 2017; the Family Report of the National Ministry for Family, Seniors, Women and Youth 2017; the 15. Children and Youth Report of German Parliament 2017; the KIGGS Study 2014; and Prognos future report family 2030[1]. During the last decades, family forms changed from the leading traditional concept of "couple with children" to ways of living together without institutional support. In today's generation, 29% live as couples without children, 26% are singles and 24% live as couples with children. This might be the result of low birth rate, combined with increasing life expectancy and more and more unpopular traditional concept (Bundesinstitut für Bevölkerungsforschung 2017).

However, the number of children in Germany is slowly growing. The birth rate increased from 1.37 children per woman in 2013 to 1.5 in 2015. Nevertheless, it is a low number compared to most European countries (Statistisches Bundesamt 2017). German family becomes an interesting subject for the future: from a prediction 2030–interrogation 2016, we get the information that 76% of participants prefer family as the most important sense of life, more important than friends, jobs and hobbies.

There are 8 out of 10 underage children who grow up with couples as parents, 7 out of 10 couples are married, and the proportion of singles is 20%. The relevance of family as a future issue also is to be seen on trade statistics and selling numbers of children's under 3 years of equipment (2.5 billion Euros which is a 5% increase compared to the year before). Eighty-five percentage out of 5000 people between 20 and 39 years postulated that it is important to have children (Bundesinstitut für Bevölkerungsforschung 2013). The requirements for modern parenthood in Germany have increased. The child's well-being and social expectation of perfect equipment also are instruments for self-fulfilment of the parent (helicopter parents) (Henry-Huthmacher 2014).

The most important purpose in life for people in Germany is family and health (Best for Planning 2013). Ninety-three percentage of parents are happy with their family life, but fathers seem to be even more happy than mothers. There is no greater influence of sociodemographic markers on satisfaction than educational background of parents, number and age of children. Couples are more satisfied than singles (45–26%). The nicest family moments are described during common meals or conversations with children.

Families with a lower educational background and singles enjoy the use of modern media with their children, and educated parents enjoy common holidays as an intensive time together. For singles, financial problems play an important role (Forschungsbericht de Sinus-Institutes 2014). In 2014, the part of employed mothers

---

[1] https://www.prognos.com/publikationen/alle-publikationen/649/show/c924f7cc5e339a89b60b5 1228db048af/

of 2–3-year-old children was 57% (in 2006 it was 41%). The part of fathers who demanded parent's money to stay with their children increased from 3.5% in 2006 to 34% in 2014 (Statistisches Bundesamt 2014). So equal partnership, ordinary education and flexibility of work-life balance, these are issues of young families in Germany today. In case of separation and divorce, there are special challenges which are shown in male and female perspective by non-profit organizations.

Developing with more working hours of parents, the needed childcare is increasing. For children aged 1–3 years in 2014, it was 33% versus 14% in 2006. Family is the first encounter of learning and teaching for children—a chance of education to work poverty (Bundesministerium für Familie, Senioren, Frauen und Jugend 2017). From the AOK Familienstudie 2014, we know that the time watching TV depends on age of children as well as their educational status. TV by now is the most important medium used in German families, and 25% of all children between 3 and 19 years of age watch TV regularly multiple times a week (Medienpädagogischer Forschungsverband Südwest 2011).

Data from year 2017 including 7.14 Mio children shows that 37% of children aged 6–9 years and 84% of those aged 10–13 years own a smartphone or mobile, although all of them mention to prefer playing with friends in nature or activities with their families. Seventy-two percentage of German children read books or magazines, having more contact to paper books than to YouTube or PlayStation (Bundesinstitut für Bevölkerungsforschung 2017).

In modern times, children have a good life in their families. They are the centre and rarely miss material things. They use modern media—especially TV and smartphones, while they do enjoy time with family and friends more. Common time is rare in working families. Health problems and behavioural disorders are new challenges. The pressure lasting on children to operate efficiently in kindergarten, in school as well as at home is bigger. However, space and time for creative games are rare.

Family models are an important part of social identity. They give orientation in life decisions related to partnership, parenthood and determining the time of starting a family (Bundesinstitut für Bevölkerungsforschung 2017). A Family Models Study in 2012 and 2016 from Meinungsforschungsinstitut included 5000 persons born between years 1973 and 1992 in a telephone survey. They were contacted several times, and in 2016, they were asked the same questions about their idea of family compared to their current family life. The consent named most when being asked for a functioning family model were a fulfilling partnership, a joyful family life including children, equality in gender as well as being able to guarantee a stable upbringing of children. In real life, those ideas change and a more differentiated picture is described. The lived reality of a family model is evolving together with the role distribution among parents when starting a family. The number of mothers continuing to work increases, just as the number of fathers staying home for parental leaves. In the majority of young families after birth of the first child, a traditional family model with a full-time working father and a part-time working mother is realized. The reduced working hours for mothers keep on as long as the children are small.

The wish to have children is a widespread desire among couples. Financial aspects just as creating a life plan affect family planning. A growing number of parents see day childcare positively. In Eastern Germany, the idea finds wider acceptance than in Western Germany. German men feel struggled by working full time and at the same time being fully present in children's education. To reconcile work with family life is a possible cause of psychosocial distress in those men.

Equal partnership, common education and good possibilities to combine private and professional work, these are themes of young families today in Germany. The social conditions are good at the moment; nevertheless, poverty of children is increasing as well as the pressure on children. Children are in the centre of families and get everything, even more they need. Others are neglected, particularly in migrant families, living in precarious life situations, and get fewer education. To encounter families in problematic situations, there are special projects in early intervention programmes and child welfare. Health prevention and more institutions of childcare are an important challenge for society and current politics as well as more financial support.

Besides best institutional childcare, financial support, optimum of new media products and best education: intensive bonding, the feeling to be loved and welcome in a family spending a lot of time together help children to develop and make their life.

2.3 The Image of the Latvian Family

Family plays a crucial role in the development of welfare, demographical vitality and the lifestyle of the nation in Latvia. Families in Latvia have changed during the past thirty years. The process can be related to rapid economic, political and social changes in Eastern Europe, starting from late 1980. At the same time, it can be related to postmodern changes in family structures in Europe and beyond.

Changing demographic structure of population by age and gender has influence of family structures and family lifestyles. The birth rate started to decrease from 1991 to 1992 and continued for almost two decades. Since 1993, the share of people at retirement age exceeds the share of children and young people, and it means that in future the number of population at working age will be smaller and the level of demographic burden will increase. Although since 2011 the share of children (0–14 years) in the total population has slightly increased due to modest rise in the birth, the proportion of working age population continuously decreases, and the share of population at retirement age increases. At the beginning of 2016, there were 377 persons at retirement age and 248 children aged under 15 per 1000 population at working age (Central Statistical Bureau of Latvia 2016).

Marriage and family formation patterns in Latvia are changing. Before 1990, young people started family rather early—for women, the average age of the first marriage was 22.2 years, and for men 24 years. Nowadays, women and men prefer to establish themselves first in the labour market before starting a family.

There have been essential changes in the dominating attitude and behaviour towards the age of the first marriage. Since 1990, the average age of first marriage has increased to age of 24.4 for women and 26.5 for men in 2000, and further increased to age of 28.7 for women and 30.8 for men in 2015 (see Fig. 2.1).

The divorce rates in Latvia are among the highest in Europe. In 1990, the number of divorces was 457 per 1000 marriages. During the following years of rapid economic and social changes, also the number of divorces has reached 666 (on 1000 marriages) in 2000. Relative economic and social stabilization since 2000 has led to decreasing number of divorces, reaching 480 divorces per 1000 marriages (Central Statistical Bureau of Latvia 2016). During the last decades, the average duration of divorced marriage has increased from 8.4 years in 1990 to 11.7 in 2000 and 13.7 in 2015. The divorced marriages had changed the lives of common 3600 underage children in 2015. Among them, the highest proportion of children influenced by their parents' divorce were in age group 5–9 (36%) and age group 10–14 (25%). With decreasing marriage rates and increasing divorce rates, there are more children growing in single-parent and blended families.

Fertility rates have been persistently low in Latvia since 1990s, which leads to smaller families. At the same time, in 2015, both the crude birth rate in Latvia (11.1) was higher than in the European Union (10.0) and higher than in the Czech Republic (10.5) and also the total fertility rate in Latvia (1.65) was higher than in EU (1.58) and higher than in the Czech Republic (1.53) (Central Statistical Bureau of Latvia 2016). Low birth rates and increasing life expectancy lead to fewer children and more grandparents than before. The number of children born within marriage in the 1990 was almost 85% and decreased to 59% in 2016. At least 16.2% of all children in Latvia are raised by cohabiting partners. However, married couples more often than single or cohabiting partners have the second and the third child. The average age of mother at birth of the first child has risen from 22.7 in 1990 to 23.9 in 2000 and to 27 in 2015. Higher age of mother at the birth of the first child can increase the probability of having fewer children than previous generations.

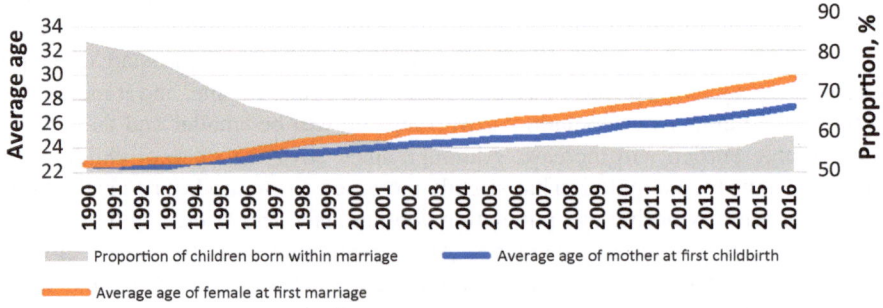

Fig. 2.1 Average age of female at marriage and childbirth, 1990–2015. *Source* Central Statistical Bureau of Latvia, Demography (2016)

The share of extramarital birth reached 44% from the total birth (2014). This indicator is higher than in the EU (40%) and somehow lower than in the Czech Republic (46.7%). The number of abortions in Latvia has decreased essentially—from 60 abortions per 1000 women aged 15–49 in 1991 to 11 abortions in 2015. This data indicates high literacy and use of contraception.

Issue of the family institution is rather topical in Latvia. The traditional family has changed, cohabitation family relations have increased in numbers and prevalence, and a term used for those relationships—"steady non-cohabiting relationships" (McGinnis 2003)—is receiving higher prevalence. However, in Latvian normative regulations, term "registered partnerships" is not used and no rights are granted to unregistered and the same-sex couples. The term "partnership" is not regulated by the Latvian legislation, although cohabiting partnerships are not new for Latvia and they exist side by side with marital relationships as a peculiar alternative to marriage. Partnerships are usually referred to the widely used term of "civil marriage". The issue of partnerships is relevant in Latvia because partnerships form a significant share of unions existing outside marriage and the number of children born in nonregistered partnerships is increasing. The topicality of partnerships in Latvia is indirectly highlighted by statistics on children born outside marriage. Survey data (2015) confirms that 72% consider it acceptable for partners to cohabit without registering a marriage.

Nuclear family consisting of two parents and children is the dominating family form in Latvia. It is seen by society as being the typical family form, which is ideal to raise children because children in nuclear families receive stability from two-parent structure and have better lifestyle opportunities because they have two parents. However, around 54% of children live in a nuclear family unit. The average size of the household is 2.4 persons. At present, the extended family—family with two or more adults, related by blood or marriage, living in the same household or home—is a rather rare phenomenon in Latvia.

Single-parent family is a type of family relations, which is rather widespread in Latvia and consists of one parent raising one or more children on her/his own. Prevalent single-parent family is a mother with her children (with 30.5% child raised by mother and 4.4% child raised by a father) (Central Statistical Bureau of Latvia 2017). There is only one earner, which limits income, access and opportunities to enjoy the lifestyle family members would love to. According to the EU-SILC data, at risk of poverty are about 37% of single-parent families.

During the recent decades, there is another subtype of family developing, mainly in the East European countries. The development of this is family type is related to the long-term economical migration of one or both parents who leave their children behind. This type of family-like relationships can be called geographically *dispersed or transnational family*. This type of family got its increase since the economic crises in Latvia (2008–2009), when many parents left the country due to long-term economical migration, leaving their children behind. According to statistics, about 259 thousand people have started economical migration. Some of them have migrated together with their children; however, more than 8 thousand children were left behind. Research on dispersed families and children left behind (Trapenciere 2011) shows that one or both parents living abroad and leaving their children behind is a risk factor to ensure the family functions (economical, socialization, education, emotional support, etc.). According to research, children left behind have been left with relatives, friends, grandparents or by children themselves. Thus, a new type of family-like relations appears, which are not defined as any type of family. The closest family type to the dispersed families is a *grandparent family*—is a family, which has taken the duty of raising their grandchildren, and the parents are not present in the child's life. For the family lifestyle description in the case of Latvia, we would like to discuss lifestyle perspectives of children left behind either in grandparent family, blended family, foster family or when left by themselves. Children left behind or "Euro-orphans" is a term, which in Latvia first was discussed in 2010, when a term Euro-orphan was introduced (Trapenciere 2011)—a child, who is left behind due to his/her parent's long-term economical migration.

The exact number of dispersed (transnational) family arrangements in Latvia or in Europe is unknown because of a scarcity of data. Reports by NGOs and UNICEF indicate that approximately 25% of children in selected migrant-sending countries have at least one parent abroad.

Family institute in Latvia had faced many changes since regaining independence in 1990: nuclear family is losing its dominating place, and cohabiting is increasing. Economical migration has developed a new model of relations between parents and their children. It can have a long-term negative effect on children. Although parental economical migration provides positive income effect in majority of cases, a negative effect is present among children due to insufficient emotional interaction, missing non-verbal communications, increased feelings of sadness/loneliness and deficiency of schoolwork support. The main problems for teenagers and adolescents occur through increased stress and social isolation. The literature reports that regardless of parental migration status, most children experience increased stress, need to take additional household responsibilities (those who are left by themselves) and faced increasing social isolation with grandparents. This situation is concerning because there can be a causal relationship between substantial stress and developing addictions, abuse or depression during adolescence.

2.4   The Image of the Polish Family

The family in its various forms, structures and functions is the universal principle of culture (Gough 1971). Observing the directions of changes in contemporary culture, we can see that the family is subject to significant changes and begins to lose its privileged position in the structures of the social world, which can be described as *a family crisis* as an institution and a primary group.

-The equally serious feature of our civilization is the already mentioned strong and still weakening of social ties, the decomposition of traditional communities in which man is involved and in which he finds support. This is not just about the family, but even more about the village community, neighbourhood communities, various cooperatives and associations. The individual is increasingly left to himself, isolated from others and from the community. Family and family lifestyles no longer have to refer in their forms and manifestations to tradition and upbringing, drawing from axiological cultural resources aimed at promoting individualism, subjectivity and dynamism captured as the endogenous tendency that has been growing since the mid-twentieth century, which is becoming a source of increasingly growing level of stress for the individual. As a consequence, hybrid forms of family life are also conceived.

Both statistical data and in-depth sociological research indicate significant and persisting tendencies in the transformations of lifestyles in Polish society, which is expressed both in attitudes towards marriage and family, and in the practices of family life.

In various studies on the axiological orientations of Polish society, the attachment to the institution of marriage and the family as a value is very strong. "More than half of Poles (54%) declare such attitudes, the same number is in favour of formalizing consensual unions, and 15% are of the opinion that people living together without marriage should necessarily get married. Poland has the lowest in the European Union (next to Greece and Malta) percentage of people (around 2%) "aged 20 plus" who live in consensual unions, while the average proportion of such unions in the European Union amounts up to around 9%. It is the highest in Sweden, namely over 18%, and in the Czech Republic it approaches the level of 6%" (Główny Urząd Statystyczny 2016a, b).

The value of the family is higher for people who have already established their own families and feel responsible for them (Wadowski 1998). Similarly, as in other European countries also in Poland the number of marriages decreases, and the so-called balance of marriages entered into and dissolved in Poland has shown a negative trend since 2000, which has its consequences also in the decline in the number of births, because more than half of the babies born each year are born during the first three years of the parents' marriage.

The number of single-parent families is also systematically increasing. In recent decades, the percentage of new marriages has decreased in the vast majority of European countries. Thus, on a European scale, apart from exceptions and also in Poland, demographers define the "tendency to enter into marriage" as a signature of lifestyles of young people, and those who make such decisions get married at the age of about 30. Despite the fact that young people consider the family to be one of the most important values, starting it is postponed for later because earlier they strive to strengthen their professional position and property status. The trends observed for several decades in the developed Western countries are explained by the increasingly late achievement of professional career readiness, as well as by the discipline of work in corporations requiring employees' availability and mobility. Similar lines of professional development of both sexes are also noteworthy, which results in a stronger competition between them. Keeping the status of "singles" is becoming more and more common. In sociological literature, there functions the concept of *basement dwellers* that refers to categories of older adolescents staying in the family home who do not become independent and are afraid of responsibility for their own decisions, and even more of the responsibility arising from entering into marriage, especially since it would be "forever". Poland is in the top ten European countries where adult children do not leave their home for a long time; for women it is about 28.5, and for men about 30 years of age. Over half of the population aged 18–34 has the status of *basement dwellers.* The percentage of *basement dwellers* (2008) in Poland was about 58%. In Slovakia, this percentage was the highest and amounted up to nearly 70%. The lowest percentage of *basement dwellers* was recorded in Denmark (about 14%), and on average in the European Union their number amounts up to around 46%. In the Czech Republic, this percentage was just over 50% (Choroszewicz and Wolff 2010).

Nationwide surveys show that almost 2/3 of Poles accept the postponement of decisions about marriage by young people, which is also associated with the approval of cohabitation.

In the perspective of sociological analyses referring to the role of language and its legitimizing functions, the conclusions of nationwide research stressing the wider social understanding (definitions) of the family are significant. In recent years, there are more and more respondents who define family as a couple living in a cohabitation and raising their child/children (from 71 to 78%) or having no children (from 26 to 33%); the number of respondents who consider gay or lesbian couples as a family who raise a child or children together (from 9 to 23%), as well as those who define family as an informal relationship of two people of the same sex who have no children (from 6 to 14%) has also significantly increased.[2]

It is symptomatic that more women distance themselves from the role of the mother (15%) than men from the role of the father (12%). This information is complemented by the conclusions from EVS research regarding the relationship between having children and satisfaction with life. The author of these analyses states, among others: "Poles' attitudes are similar to the attitudes of Eastern Europeans in the sense that having children decreases, and does not increase their level of life satisfaction, moreover, children do not compensate for the lack of a partner for either women or men. In the case of people living in relationships, the negative impact of children on the level of satisfaction is felt weaker by women than men, which is a result characteristic of Poland" (Konieczna-Sałamatin 2013).

In the light of changes in value orientation, the CBOS survey is interesting, which stresses that almost two-fifths of respondents (37%) believe that if people love and trust each other, their marital status is of little importance. Few respondents are

---

[2]"In the era of intense changes, also the basic social unit, which is the family, is subject to various transformations. Preferred and implemented models of family life are changing, intra-family relationships are transforming, and finally the understanding of the family itself is not as unambiguous as it used to be. Among others, it is a consequence of an increase in the number of divorces and separations, as well as the number of single parents, delaying matrimonial decisions, abstaining from procreation or abandonment of the idea of having children, an increase in the number of single households or the growing popularity of informal relationships, whose rights are sought by some social circles. One thing does not change: the family, however understood, still has great significance for Poles and is the basic value of their everyday life." Family—its contemporary meaning and understanding. CBOS. BS.33/2013. /Centrum Badania Opinii Społecznej/Centre for Public Opinion Research. Warsaw, March 2013, p. 1.

against the legalization of relationships (5%) or have no opinion on the subject (4%). However, we also see that in many cases cohabitation takes on the status of permanent relationships. Cohabiting couples are more often formed by persons with a relatively lower level of education, lower wages or the ones who are unemployed. Many couples bring up children by taking advantage of disability and social benefits, rent houses more often in poor technical and civilization conditions, and earn a livelihood by working in the grey zone or migrating abroad. Less than half of the respondents (49%) reject the model of life "without a stable partner", and more than two-fifths (44%) accept it. Most Poles (61%) also deny that the life of a single person is more attractive than that of a person in a stable relationship.

An important feature of the Polish families' lifestyles is the inclusion of religious weddings in marriage designs. This is connected with universally declared religious-ness and relatively high rates of religious practices. Nevertheless, the number of religious weddings shows a declining tendency. For example, if in the year 2000 the percentage of church weddings was 72%, in 2016, it amounted up to 63% (Główny Urząd Statystyczny 2016a, b). CBOS research shows that more than a quarter of respondents (28%) recognize the primacy of a concordat wedding, i.e. an ecclesias-tical celebration with legal effects, and a similar proportion (27%) admit that although civil marriage is sufficient, spouses should also have a church wedding. About 9% of respondents think that a religious marriage is not important, while every third respondent (33%) does not attach much importance to these matters. In some cities, for example, in Warsaw and Wałbrzych, only civil marriages (in civil registries) are entered into more often than religious ones. Religious (concordat)[3] marriages are an important expression not only of religious attitudes but also of acceptance of cultural traditions. The declining rates of religious marriages point to the scale of the secular-ization of the lifestyle of young people. The declining marriage rate correlates with the increasing percentage of extramarital births and the phenomenon of cohabitation of couples in matrimonial and reproductive age. Countries with low marriage rates have high rates of extramarital births. Since the mid-1980s, the number of children that come into the world beyond the traditionally perceived family has been on a systematic increase. The percentage of extramarital births increased from around 5% in the first half of the 1980s to nearly 16% in 2004, over 21% in 2012 and over 25% in 2016: the percentage is higher in cities (over 27%) and lower in rural areas (around 22%). The growing fertility rate results from the increase in cohabitation and the growth of incomplete families (mainly single mothers). In some large cities (e.g. Łódź), it exceeds 30%, and in poviats (e.g. Gryfice) it reaches half of all births. The highest percentages of extramarital births in Poland occur in West Pomerania, in the voivodeship of Lubuskie, in the border area of Lower Silesia and the north-western part of Warmia and Mazury. Children brought to the world by teenagers,

---

[3]"Concordat" marriages are religious marriages entered into in Poland under the Concordat signed between the Republic of Poland and the Holy See in 1993. Religious marriages are also entered into under agreements between other churches and Religious Associations and the Government of the Republic of Poland.

whose percentage, for example, in 2002 was 14.5% and in 2010 amounted up to 9.8%, have its share in this phenomenon (Brzozowska 2011).

Fast-growing birth rates in Poland can be treated as socially relevant indicators of changes in lifestyles and value orientation showing the scale of the redefinition of the cultural significance of marriage and the family. Low rates of birth are of similar importance. Since 1989, Poland has experienced the period of birth rate decrease (Główny Urząd Statystyczny 2016a, b), and long-term forecasts (2060) show a dramatic social situation in which there will be 670 pensioners per 1.000 people in the working age. Against the background of the European Union, Poland is one of the countries with the lowest intensity of births. According to Eurostat data, in 2015 the lower fertility rate than in Poland (1.32) was recorded only in Portugal (1.31). The highest fertility rate is currently recorded in the countries of Western and Northern Europe; the highest was in France (1.96) and Ireland (1.92). In the Czech Republic, the birth rate was 1.57. "It should be noted that all of these coefficients remain below the value referred to as simple generational replacement, which is 2.13–2.15" (Główny Urząd Statystyczny 2016a, b).

Sociological research shows a large "fertility potential", which is expressed by declarations regarding the desire to have children. CBOS research shows that there are "only 4%" of people who do not want to have children at all, and 10% of people who want to have one child. The remaining part, namely over 80%, would like to have two or three children (a total of almost 75%). According to data published in 2017 by the Polish Association of Large Families "Trzy Plus" ("Three Plus"), 627 thousand mothers bring up three or more children. The most numerous group are mothers with three children, namely 74%, four children are raised by 14% of mothers, 7% of mothers have five children, and 5% even more. The data shows that 68% of mothers with many children are professionally active, and most of them work full time. According to the "Trzy Plus" Association, in large families there is a partnership division between everyday duties; both women and men do housework such as washing, cleaning and cooking. In large families, 84% of mothers chose a formalized union, 64% of women got married in church, 20% had a civil ceremony, and only 10% live in a free relationship. Most mothers who have large families live in villages and small towns, and their number is the smallest in the largest cities.

One may recall a lot of statistical data, more or less describing in detail the styles of modern family life. Statistics only indicate numbers, but behind the numbers there are deep transformations in culture and in social mentality taking place.

Numerous sociological studies conducted in Poland stress a relatively stable triad of basic axiological orientations which are built on the pillars of the value of family, friends and children. It also includes health aspects (Świątkiewicz 2013). The future of marriage and family, familiarness as a way of life, will depend on the ability to defend the privileged status of a natural family and to renew its attractiveness as an emotional community that legitimizes the identity of the cultural code of Polish society.

2.5 The Image of the Slovakian Family[4]

A nation's character, its peculiarity and uniqueness are directly related to its traditions and its culture, which usually stems from the traditions. The ideal of a Slovak family is highly disparate. It is variously based on very different religious (where there are differences even among Christians), traditionalist, the so-called postmodern, "rainbow" or even partisan ideas. A generally accepted notion of future families may only emerge on the basis of an examination of intergenerational relations, i.e. a specific, interdisciplinary field, which has so far absented in the creation of family policy.

The notion of the future of families can only arise out of a real understanding of contemporary family life and the factors that influence it. What, then, is Slovak family like?

Singly's observation is also valid in case of Slovak families. According to it:

1. There is a greater dependence of families on state.
2. There is a greater independence on relatives.
3. There is a greater independence of spouses on family (Singly 1999).

These statements are considered an initial hypothesis also in case of family life in Slovakia.

In comparison with the lifestyle of other families in the Central Europe, in Slovakia, significant differences (certain peculiarities) appear between lives of urban and rural families. More importantly, family lives are differed by their economic situation. According to Anton Michálek (2010, 14), in Slovakia: "… income, salaries and poverty are highly differentiated regionally, meaning that their values and the level of inequality are also determined geographically… there is a type of research, in which space function as the dominant dimension… Unfortunately, in Slovak as well as Czech literature, studies of geographical aspects of income, salaries and poverty (of families)… are largely absent". Michálek provides an accurate analysis of low-income communities and their numbers in individual Slovak district, and of the distribution of employees according to industry, including the index of poverty. The provided characteristics that have not undergone an empirical research so far also include the fact that a third of Slovak families are financially supported by their members from abroad. The financial support of families in Slovakia is provided by workers from the Czech Republic, Great Britain and Northern Ireland as well as by people employed in Austria, Germany, Italy, Switzerland, Ireland, Netherlands and France, which finalizes the top ten countries (available at https://ekonomika.sme.sk/c/20135851/tretine-ludom-na-slovensku-pomaha-financne-rodina-zo-zahranicia.html#ixzz4q5QADD3X, 18.8.2017).

Importantly, Slovak family and, consequently, the course of Slovak society are characterized by demographic development. According to demographic studies (Vaňo et al. 2009), over the last two decades, the structure of Slovak family has been changing. According to the aforementioned authors, the development of population after the year 2000 has been characterized by a gradual stabilization of trends that

---

[4]This paper was also published in Slovak (Ondrejkovič 2018).

have followed a period of important changes at the end of the previous century. This stabilization is oriented towards a new model of reproductive and family behaviour, which should fully assert itself once the period of transformation ends. The years 2005 and 2006 brought a few surprises, especially regarding the development of birth and marriage rate, while in years 2007 and 2008, the expected trends were confirmed virtually to their full extent. Marriage and birth rate increased, the divorce rate continued to grow, but it was apparent it was nearing its ceiling, abortion rate grew slightly smaller, mortality continued to decrease and net migration rate increased. The increases in birth rate and net migration rate were crucial here. The influence of demographic development on increase in population and age distribution also corresponded to the expectations—the drop of natural increase has (temporarily) stopped, and population ageing has continued at an increased rate.

Vaňo et al. (2009) also mention that according to the chart of marriage rate among single people, the greatest decrease of marriage rate occurred in males below 25 years of age, while there has also been a drop in the group of 25–29-year-olds. The greatest change, however, occurred in the group of 20–24-year-olds, in which the probability of a single person entering marriage dropped by more than 60%, while at age 20–23, it was almost 75%. In the female population, the decrease in marriage rate between 1996 and 2008 was the most significant at age 17–21, where it decreased by more than 60%.

The development of marriage rate seemed the least stable, as it was impossible to eliminate various courses or an unsteady progress. In the present, in fact, we are unable to estimate reliably how the population, especially the current young generation, is going to react to cohabitation, i.e. whether it will continue to consider it a temporary relationship of partners that is going to be followed by marriage, or whether cohabitation will become recognized as a permanent form of partnership to a larger degree.

It should be noted that many initial hypotheses assume that the trend of unmarried partner relationships, which appears in growing numbers in many developed democratic countries in Europe, will also impact Slovakia. A poll examining family behaviour of university graduates in Slovakia showed that more than a half of respondents (56.5%) considered unmarried cohabitation a convenient test prior to marriage. As much as 16.8% of respondents even perceived cohabitation as a better form of partner relationship than formal marriage (Mládek and Siročková 2004). According to these authors, in 1991, there were 20,864 cohabitations in Slovakia, with a ratio of 100 married people to 1.65 people living in a cohabitation. By 2001, this value increased to 30,466 cohabitations (2.68 people in cohabitation to 100 married individuals). The present study assumes that by 2017, this number doubled and that it will continue to grow in future. The studies of changes in the composition of cohabitating individual in Slovakia (Džambazovič and Šprocha 2017) advanced closer to the actual situation, when they started to look for causes of the growing number of cohabitations primarily in the changes of values and preferences related to the increasing individualism, secularization and equality within families, followed by the changes in objective conditions, including the overall increase in uncertainty and changes in the job market. According to the census of inhabitants, houses and flats in

Slovakia in 2011, the greatest tendency to cohabitation appeared among individuals who attained the lowest education, declared Roma nationality and lived in urban environments.

In an international conference on social and legal protection of children and social guardian ship, Špániková (2015) noted in relation to contemporary family that until recently, Slovak family was a comparatively stable unit, while in the present, it is more open, i.e. less formally bound by marriage, contracts or legal verdicts. "Family no longer possesses formal attributes; rather, it is based on more or less voluntary principles and emotional closeness. This also causes conflicts, because if the partners lack an emotional understanding, it gives rise to tensions and break-ups. However, when family relations used to be linked to a formal agreement (wedding), this agreement was binding and kept the family together in some way". This suggests Slovak families are currently governed by emotions. "However, when emotions are exhausted and worries and troubles arise, where there is no longer a good atmosphere in the family, partners split and families break up". Consequently, according to Špániková, new partnerships emerge in the form of stepfamilies. "In the past, families were closed units and partners attempted to resolve hardships and troubles that appeared in the marriage. In the present, however, partners frequently quit the relationship, while their children frequently remain lacking both financial and social securities. This mostly puts a strain on the mother, who has to provide for children in terms of finances, social aspects and upbringing".

Džambazovič (2016, 2017) provides a very different depiction of contemporary Slovak family. In his view, both administrative surveys and sociological research point at an apparent transformation of behaviour in the Slovak family over the last 25 years. It pertains to both quantitative and qualitative aspects of reproductive and partnership behaviour. The changes were very intense, and over a relatively short period, the family behaviour that stabilized in the "golden age of family" in 1970s and 1980s was "overwritten". The unified progression of family life was disrupted, and a clear and cohesive timing of life events was abandoned. Gradually, several flexible models of reproductive and family behaviour emerged. This resulted in a huge diversity in the progression of family and personal life of Slovak citizens as well as in the notions about the course of life and the timing of specific transitions.

The Slovak specifics also include a similarity to the type of family structure prevalent in Southern European countries, which, however, raises some doubts. Džambazovič also considers the Southern European model to be the most appropriate one for the Slovak situation regarding the passage into adulthood. In this model, it is typical that children stay longer with their parents, while their moving out is mostly prevented by economic factors. He compares the process of gaining independence on parents to Poland (46% in 2008), Hungary (51.2% in 2008) and the Czech Republic (52.5% in 2008), where there is not possible, however, to prove the "Southern European model". The specificity of the Slovak situation is also apparent in the high share of extended households as well as in their structure and in gaining one's own housing. Frequently, leaving parents is only connected to a wedding or to a foundation of family.

On the basis of empirical researches performed by the VEGA agency, the contemporary, "modern" Slovak family appeared lacking in cohesion, **consistency**, stability and even sustainability; when dealing with more profound obstacles and problems, *relations within the family become* **chaotic** as their structure changes frequently, which often induces *feelings of helplessness*. The function of social control provided by family disappears or is reduced. Features of contemporary family life can also be characterized by aspects of anomie. In this regard, it is necessary to take note of specific functional and dysfunctional effects of deviations of family life, life satisfaction in a given family, attainment of social capital and affiliation to religions and churches. The present findings are based on an interpretation of data collected via a survey that was primarily focused on examining intergenerational relations. These changes, designated here as elements of anomie in the family, are accompanied by other social phenomena, including:

- Increase in family violence;
- Frequent syndrome of neglected and abused child[5];
- Changes in roles within family;
- Changes in male and female social status;
- The sometimes almost schizoid role of a mother who decides between professional career and motherhood;
- Excessive strain on all family members, especially women.

The present study proposes a hypothesis that it is due to the aforementioned phenomena that there is a frequent (and growing) unwillingness to bring children into the world.

In conclusion, it is possible to note that the development of Slovak family has in the past decade been characterized by a combination of historical continuity and important changes. Among young families (young generation), a combination of traditional and postmodern values and ways of life is also prevalent. The present study proposes an ideological hypothesis that Slovak family life is situated between a continuity and a change, i.e. a quality that should be empirically described in terms of its aspects and attributes, and further examined; subsequently, however, it should also be evaluated, so that we do not merely observe this development idly. It is considered inevitable to attempt to positively influence this development on the basis of the results of the evaluation on a macro-scale (especially in terms of creating an adequate and goal-oriented family policy free of a vulgar economism), but also on a microscale, via social pedagogy, social work, counselling, regional, education and communal family policy, activizing all concerned parties, including science and research.

---

[5]The issue of child abuse and neglect has been discussed from the perspective of social pathology by Vlčková, M. in Ondrejkovič, P. et al.: Sociálna patológia, Bratislava: Veda, publ. by SAV, 2001.

2.6 The Image of the Ukrainian Family

All the time, family was based on the Ukraine society and its essential part, makes influence on all aspects of social life. As integral part of society, family accomplishes important social, ethnocultural functions, which connect it with all spheres of human life. Accordingly, it is attraction of different sciences (sociology, demography, economy, psychology, pedagogics, medicine). Each of discipline has a body of knowledge in various family research approaches and its aspects. Pedagogues and psychologists focus especially on topics related to family upbringing, forming family values or development of family super substantiality as a reflexion of society.

As a social phenomenon, the Ukraine family went through many hardships. Archaeological researches and written sources of Kyiv Rus age, in particular "Rusjka Pravda" of Yaroslav the Wise, show existence of monogamy family (one husband has one wife) from territory from time of its settlement. Such a type of family is most typical today. Sociologists divide monogamy family into "traditional" and "extended". Another type of traditional and extended family is "a family community", which consists of one married couple with children and other relatives (wife's or husband's father, their sisters or brothers.) This type of family has been exciting for a long time.

Archaeologists approve the existence in the Ukraine's territory from Late Stone Age (35–40) different types of families: traditional, extended, communities. From time to time, they have been transformed: traditional families transferred to extended or communities, or extended family changed in one-parented family. Otherwise it was typical for the Ukrainians to live separately. This is explained by particular psychological features and individuality of national mentality: Ukrainian people consider liberty, private property, households on smallest part of ground as the best of their value.

Generalization of sociological researches gives opportunity to distinguish such specialities of modern Ukrainian family.

- Transformation of parents and children values. Modern young people changed their minds about charity, now deceived. In value system of modern young family tendency to becoming wealth, upbringing pragmatic, rational, willed, successful children prevail. Kindness, skills to commiserate and help another people often are underestimated.
- Separation of young from extended family. In modern times it is an objective process, which is determined by social-economic development of society. Young families tend to self-appraisal, do not take into consideration adult experience, do not develop family traditions and keep everyday difficulties and professional problems. These all factors have negative effects on children's upbringing process in family.
- Reduction processes in family. Decrease in birth is caused by rivalry increasing of job hunting, marriage processes, increasing of money spending on upbringing, bad household conditions and selfish tendency of parents "to live for themselves".

Reducing of one-child family causes detachment from children because they do not have an example of care and honour to other people.

- Reduction of positive effect of social environment to family development. Urbanization of society, pragmatism of life, lack of family communication; so, moral example on base of state human policy transforms system of life priorities and family values.
- Misunderstanding by parents' system of forming human relationships with children, limitation of relations within household. Sometimes, parents depreciate moral and psychological relations in family, mutual respect, care. Harmony of family upbringing depends on sincereness and honesty of love to children. Children cannot develop within advance feeling, and they want to be loved now and such as individuals.
- Expansion of non-traditional marriage relations—unregistered marriage. Economic difficulties, problems in job hunting, and uncertainty in future disrupted the civil marriage. Some of people living in unregistred marriages consider civil marriage as preparedness to family life, display of self –liberty or source of serving romantic relations. Other people consider that such type of family causes distrust and instability.

Such features of Ukraine family we consider as critical, which cause development of dysfunctions, are: increasing of dynamic of divorces, decreasing of birth rate, birth children of unwed parents, increasing of family conflicts, frustration; decline of material and spiritual prosperity.

As Khyzhna and Kondratyeva (2016) consider, there is an urgent need to reform educational system according to the current trends of society to protect children from negative influence. Solution of this problem requires such vulnerable children as homeless, neglected children, "street children", social orphans, and 93.4% from them are temporary migrants.

According to material of Justice Ministry (https://usr.minjust.gov.ua/ua/freese arch), previous year there were rare marriage and more divorces. In 2016, 229.45 thousand of new families were registered, and it was 69.6 of thousand less than in 2015. Number divorce on previous year became more than 1.2 thousand (35.46 thousand in 2016 according 34.2 thousand in 2015). Experts are assured that such statistic is a result of unbalanced social–economical and moral orientations in Ukraine.

Researches presented by Ukrainian sociologists, demographics and psychologists allow to appreciate contemporary state functioning of critical Ukraine family. Results of scientific researches provide emphasizing of tendentious of functioning Ukrainian family:

- More popular are becoming incomplete, non-marital families.
- Most men and women consciously do not get married, but for satisfaction connect with sexual partner but not for family building.
- Material and rational motives of family building dominate.
- Young marriages have tendency to have only one child.

- Young marriages have inadequate demands to partner and family, which cause family rejection and actualization in professional activity.
- More marriage couples are not able to cooperate and find ways of normalizing relations, and they are not skilled in solving problems. All these factors create divorce as an instrument of deciding family conflicts.
- Most young people are oriented to encore wedding and extramarital relations in case of unhappy alliance.

Supplied tendencies confirm positive aspects of old family model are not functioned, and new norms are not prepared. Situation of breaking family, inability to adapt to life changes and increasing of personal isolation demands help and create immediate actions from state government, deputes, scientists, pedagogues and people who consider family as social value. Whereas social and people relations became severe and pragmatic, family must be a symbol of inward and economic revival of the Ukrainian state. Revival of tradition, high status of Ukrainian family, its authority, which is based on fidelity, sincere love to children and their upbringing, honour to parents and mutual understanding in family—formula to success of recovery and improvement of Ukrainian nation.

Basic vector of recovery for Ukrainian family should be a confirmation of the system of human values in kindness, wisdom, love, which goes along with a spiritual development. To inwardness of these values (according researches of V. Andrushenko, I. Beh, I. Zazyun, S. Honcharenko, A. Maslow) it is important to develop a positive perception of world, meaning and goal of life, recognition of specific family values.

Psychological, pedagogical researches of phenomena of "inwardness" consider in the context of substantial human characteristics, matter of being, moral measurement of well-being, necessity for self-improvement. Term "inwardness", as Rudnitska (2005) defines, is expressed by treasure of eternal human world, development of emotional, intellectual features, engaging to cultural value. Shevchenko (2006) considers "human inwardness" as acquirement of sense-human values and goals as permanent top of personal values and their realization in practice. As M. Berdiaev considers, "inwardness" is the best human achievement, goal and result of life. Inwardness is based on human and society eternal world, family. In time of social crisis, problem of inward development becomes national important. History approves that perish of all civilizations began from degradation of people inwardness. So, today is important to guide young family on inward values on base of kindness, respectability, honour, evil opposition for avoiding separate society, saving and development of Ukrainian family traditions as a part of society. Future of Ukraine depends on inward ideals and culture demand; interesting will be fulfilled life of each family.

Principle tradition in Ukrainian family was labour, where each member has to work, even the child. He takes part in household duties. Distribution of household duties among family members, contributes to a forming of conscientious, mutual help and respect in family. Children which grow in family where labour is respected become successful and good professional in future.

Great importance for child upbringing and development inwardness in family are aesthetical traditions, which unite all family members to save comfort and create beauty and quietness at home and outdoors.

Aesthetical traditions of forming family inwardness actualize necessity in communication with art. Art is initiation of universal inward values. Moreover as a complicated form of world inquiring, art creates, saves and transfers; accumulates the inward experience of generations in art images and influences by them human consciousness. Visiting theatre, concert halls and art exhibitions with all family members determine communication, creative thinking, feelings interchange, so is forming inward human and family sphere.

The world of art is huge and different. Music, choreography, poems and literature, art and graphic, architecture and sculpture were formed by characteristic features of art images and methods of reality description. But the main idea is creating word values, which were formed during several centuries. Realness, beauty and all values are expressed in art literature. Communication with art is forming of these values of all family members.

Nevertheless, in each family there are priorities in communication with art, dominating one of these varieties. Scientific works of Rudnitska (2005) or Khyzhna (2015) argued comprehensive apprehension of art regulates by necessity of recipient in communication with art images, which actualized problem of human relation to art–aesthetical values, conscious of self-emotional feelings of art, individual appreciation of art images.

These actualize importance of considering value criticized in art communication, which is connected with their varieties (music, art, choreography, literature and theatre), definite genders and style directions. Value criticism is provided by art orientations as awarded attitude of person to art images, their feelings. Art orientations are linked with elements of psychological direction (interests, tastes, necessities, directions) and reflect definite art experience, which approved by different levels of aesthetical relations and dominations in art sphere. Art takes important role in forming of inward family ideals. Communication with art images, taking part in artistic activity, improves human and family mental world.

So, forming of contemporary inward Ukrainian family depends on social and psychological factors. As a result, the concept of family is formed by parents' influences on features of young family relation. So, it is necessary to save and care about family traditions of future generations.

Indicative for Ukrainian family are human features and functions: ethnos reconstruction—birth and upbringing children; economical–productive function connected with household; intimate–psychological function—care of special relations with relatives, parents, children; and cultural–genial: transfers of labour skills, features of cultural household traditions of nation, aesthetical necessity, capability for self-creation.

Finally, inwardness of Ukrainian family and best traditions of family upbringing can contribute to a success of future generations. For the Ukraine, it means independence, economic and political stability and high international authority. Ukrainian family must be a base and symbol inward and economic reconstruction, and goal of human activity of the Ukrainian state.

References

Best for Planning. (2013). https://gik.media/best-4-planning/. Accessed May 8, 2017.

Brzozowska, Z. (2011). Przestrzenne zróżnicowanie urodzeń pozamałżeńskich w Polsce w latach 2002–2010. *Studia Demograficzne, 2*(160), 59–84.

Bundesinstitut für Bevölkerungsforschung. (2013). https://www.bib.bund.de/Publikation/2013/Bev oelkerungsentwicklung-2013-Daten-Fakten-Trends-zum-demografischen-Wandel.html?nn=975 1912.

Bundesinstitut für Bevölkerungsforschung. (2017). Kinder-Medien-Studie. https://www.kinder-medien-studie.de/?page_id=244. Accessed April 4, 2018.

Bundesministerium für Familie, Senioren, Frauen und Jugend. (2017). Familien Report 2017. https://www.bmfsfj.de/blob/jump/119524/familienreport-2017. Accessed May 4, 2018.

Central Statistical Bureau of Latvia. (2016). Demography 2016. https://www.csb.gov.lv/en/statis tics/statistics-by-theme/population/number-and-change/search-in-theme/5-demography-2016. Accessed June 18, 2017.

Central Statistical Bureau of Latvia. (2017). Children in Latvia 2017. https://www.csb.gov.lv/en/ statistics/search?keyword=Children+in+Latvia. Accessed July 4, 2018.

Choroszewicz, M., & Wolff, P. (2010). Population and social condition. *Eurostat Statistics in Focus, 50*, 1.

de Singly, F. (1999). *Sociologie současné rodiny*. Praha: Portál.

Džambazovič, R. (2016). S kým žijeme v jednej domácnosti? Meniace sa formy rodinného správania na Slovensku z pohľadu štruktúry domácností. *Slovenská štatistika a demografia, 26*(1), 29–47.

Džambazovič, R., & Šprocha, B. (2017). Kto žije v kohabitáciách na Slovensku? *Sociológia, 49*(4), 341–460.

Forschungsbericht de Sinus-Institutes. (2014). AOK Familienstudie. https://www.aok.de/pk/filead min/user_upload/Universell/05-Content-PDF/AOK-Familienstudie-2014_Gesamtbericht-Band-1.pdf. Accessed March 15, 2017.

Główny Urząd Statystyczny. (2016a). *Marriage and fertility in Poland* (p. 12). Warsaw: Główny Urząd Statystyczny.

Główny Urząd Statystyczny. (2016b). *Population. Status, structure and natural movement in a territorial cross-section in 2016* (p. 35). Status on 31.XII.

Gough, K. (1971). The origin of the family. *Journal of Marriage and the Family, 33,* 760–771.

Henry-Huthmacher, C. (2014). *Familienleitbilder in Deutschland*. Berlin: Konrad Adenauer Stiftung.

Khyzhna, O. (2015). Pedagogical potential of Ukrainian family: Realities and perspectives. In *Issues of contemporary family in the international context* (pp. 89–117). Hradec Králové: Gaudeamus.

Khyzhna, O., & Kondratyeva, O. (2016). Preparation of social workers to work with teachers in the field of family support in the context of the present uncertain in Ukraine. In *Social work in uncertain time* (pp. 268–273). Hradec Králové: Gaudeamus.

Konieczna-Sałamatin, J. (2013). Children as a factor of family happiness. Poles against the Europeans from the East and the West. In A. Jasińska-Kania (Ed.), *Change values. Transformation of Poles' attitudes in uniting Europe* (p. 61). Warsaw: Wydawnictwo Naukowe SHOLAR.

Kraus, B. (2008). *Základy sociální pedagogiky*. Praha: Portál.

Kraus, B., & Jedličková, I. (2007). National report from the Czech Republic, University of Hradec Králové. In Z. Benkö (Ed.), *Tradition and modernity in the life-style of the families of the Visegrad countries*. Szeged: SZEK J. Gyula Higher Education Publisher.

Kučírek, J. (2014). Sociální systém rodina: geneze patologie. In T. Raszková (Ed.), *Acta sociopathologica.* Hradec Králové: Gaudeamus.

Macháčková, J. (2008). Změna sociální situace rodiny s příchodem dítěte. In *Kontakt* (Vol. 10/1, pp. 67–71). České Budějovice.

Matějček, Z., & Dytrich, Z. (1997). *Radosti a strasti prarodičů, aneb když máme vnoučata.* Praha: Grada.

McGinnis, S. L. (2003). Cohabiting, dating, and perceived costs of marriage: A model of marriage entry. *Journal of Marriage and Family, 65*(1), 105–116.

Medienpädagogischer Forschungsverband Südwest. (2011). FIM-studie 2011. https://www.mpfs.de/fileadmin/files/Studien/FIM/2011/Studie/FIM2011.pdf. Accessed March 20, 2017.

Mendelová, E. (2014). Súčasná postmoderná rodina a vnútrorodinná deľba práce. *Sociální pedagogika, 1,* 11–20.

Michálek, A. (2010). Sociálne nerovnosti a chudoba na Slovensku. Regionálna analýza.

Mládek, J., & Širočková, J. (2004). Kohabitácie ako jedna z foriem partnerského spolužitia obyvateľstva Slovenska. In *Sociológia* (Vol. 36/5, pp. 423–454).

Ondrejkovič, P. (2018). Súčasná slovenská rodina. In *Pedagogika.SK* (Vol. 9, pp. 5–17).

Rudnitska, O. (2005). Педагогіка: загальна та мистецька: Навчальний посібник/О. П. Рудницька. Тернопіль: Навчальна книга «Богдан».

Shevchenko, G. (2006). Духовність та духовна культура особистості. *Формування духовної культури учнівської молоді засобами мистецтва* (pp. 3–38). Луганськ: Вид-во СНУ ім. В.Даля.

Španiková, J. (2015). Slovenská rodina za posledné dve desaťročia mení svoju štruktúru. https://www.teraz.sk/slovensko/slovenska-rodina-zmeny-struktura/162422-clanok.html. Accessed April 12, 2016.

Statistisches Bundesamt. (2014). Sonderauswertung des Mikrozensus. https://www.destatis.de/DE/Themen/Gesellschaft-Umwelt/Bevoelkerung/Migration-Integration/_inhalt.html?__blob=publicationFile. Accessed March 15, 2017.

Statistisches Bundesamt. (2017). Eurostat. https://www.destatis.de/Europa/DE/Home/_inhalt.html. Accessed May 24, 2018.

Świątkiewicz, W. (2013). Between family and public life—Continuity and change in value orientation. In L. Adamczuk, E. Firlit, & W. Zdaniewicz (Eds.), *Socio-religious attitudes of Poles in 1991–2012* (pp. 185–206). ISKK SAC: Warsaw.

Tomášek, M. (2006). Singles a jejich vztahy; kvalitativní pohled na nesezdané a nekohabitující jednotlivce v České republice. *Sociologickj5 časopis/Czech Sociological Review, 42*(1), 81–106.

Trapenciere, I. (2011). *Euroorphans in Latvia.* Riga.

Vágnerová, M. (2007). *Vj5vojová psychologie II.: dospělost a stáří.* Praha: Karolinum.

Vaňo, B. (Ed.), Jurčová, D., Mészáros, J., Potančoková, M., & Šprocha, B. (2009). *Populačnj5 vývoj v Slovenskej republike.* Bratislava: Infostat.

Wadowski, D. (1998). *Basics and nature of social ties in the region of Central and Eastern Poland* (Ph. D. thesis), KUL, Lublin, p. 148.

Chapter 3
Socioeconomic Situation and Satisfaction in the Family Life

Abstract In this chapter, the attention is paid to two fields which are linked with family lifestyle. The first one concerns socioeconomic situations in a family and shows that the economic side of family functioning is actually very essential these days. The importance of family economic situation is affirmed also in the results of our international survey. We asked what was the main family income, experience with unemployment and whether our respondents had possibility to save some money. Furthermore, we were interested in expenditure items and in evaluation of an overall standard of living by respondents. The Germans and then Czechs evaluated it as the best, the worst was found in families in Latvia. The second part monitors life satisfaction as a subjective feeling of well-being and is understood as a part of quality of life. To the question "How do you imagine a satisfied family?", the most frequent response was—harmonic coexistence without conflicts, well-being, good health of all family members and material security. For the question "What do you lack to your satisfaction?" respondents stated—financial security and lack of free time for the family. However, there were specific differences among individual surveyed countries.

Keywords Family · Economic function · Social support · Education · Employment · Housing · Diet · Satisfaction

3.1 Characteristics of the Socioeconomic Situation of Families

Among other things, family also has an economic function. This means that family members are involved in productive and non-productive sphere during the performance of their job, but also that family as a whole becomes an important consumer the current market depends on. Furthermore, within a family system, a number of decisions are made regarding the use of material and financial means, investments and expenses.

According to economists, family members behave like consumers, comparing their income to others and determining their own consumption on this basis. The insatiable market, however, increases their consumption via advertising, forcing them

© The Author(s) 2020
B. Kraus et al., *Contemporary Family Lifestyles in Central and Western Europe*,
SpringerBriefs in Sociology, https://doi.org/10.1007/978-3-030-48299-2_3

to buy luxury goods presented by VIP celebrities and offering loans to families so that they are able to buy these goods. This means a large portion of households is experiencing financial problems that are difficult to solve. The debt of Czech households to banks and financial institutions has in the present exceeded one trillion Czech crowns.

The present study also noted that the level of material consumption determines the quality of life. Family's material situation represents the quantitative dimension of lifestyle. It is the economic situation of a family that establishes the objective factors of lifestyle. The economic situation determines both work and spare time activities.

Work activities are crucial. Work functions as a basic means of self-fulfilment, provides the most opportunities to experience success and is a source of a family's financial security. In an absence of this function, there is hardship, a decrease in living standard and quality of life, and a negative impact on lifestyle (Kraus et al. 2015).

In the present, however, it is possible and increasingly frequent that work damages family life. The last study values, attitudes, behaviour in the European Social Survey project performed by the Institute of Sociology of the Czech Academy of Sciences shows that 80% of Czech males and 61% of females sometimes feel exhausted after work to such a degree they can no longer do what they would like to at home. Exhaustion and worries related to work that need to be addressed, not enough time for the family together with a permanent fear of losing the job—that is how a third of economically active citizens perceive the influence of employment on their family lives. Furthermore, almost 64% of men and 66% of women deal with work problems at home in their spare time. On the other hand, 33% of men and 35% of women sometimes find it hard to concentrate on work because of family obligations. Coordinating work and family life seems increasingly difficult.

The economic function of family impacts already its founding. According to experts from the Czech Statistical Office, behaviour of the current young generation is influenced both by the changing values of contemporary society, and more importantly, by the current economic situation. The low share of employed people aged 25 and younger points, among other things, at an insufficient coordination of studies and work.

Starting a family requires a certain basic income. Especially among young people, however, there has been a marked decrease in real earnings in the past years. Founding a family and having a child leads to a significant decrease in the household's income, especially if the man works and the woman is on maternity leave. However, single parents are the most imperilled group. In their case, low household income is combined with a limited option of part-time jobs. This means that the worsened situation at job market together with the expected provision of income by one family member only creates less than ideal conditions to start a family. Another consequence of the socioeconomic situation is that in some cases, highly qualified women focus on career instead of having a child, causing natality to be dependent on groups with a lower (low) socioeconomic status.

Table 3.1 Standard of living in households

	Czech Republic	Poland	Hungary	Slovakia
Very good	4	12	0	2
Good	32	29	13	21
Neither good nor bad	42	45	46	50
Bad	17	8	30	20
Very bad	5	6	9	6
Does not know	0	0	2	1

In this respect, the social policy in a given society seems important. Even though the conceptions in individual surveyed countries differ, especially in terms of content, the general goal of social policy is to provide pre-emptive arrangements and to resolve existing dangerous and inappropriate living conditions and situations of disadvantaged social groups.

In June 2013, the Centre for the Research of Public Opinion (CVVM) examined how parents assessed material living conditions in household (Červenka 2013). In the same period, a similar survey was conducted in Poland, Hungary and Slovakia. At first, the respondents (in the Czech survey, 1023 respondents selected using quota sampling) answered the question about *what they think about the current economic situation of their country*. In case of Poland, where the evaluation returned the most positive results, the share of negative assessments was just under a half (47%), while one in seven (14%) Polacks gave a very positive assessment. Hungary placed send, with economic situation considered good by 6% and bad by 55% of participants. The results in the Czech Republic and Slovakia were very similar, as the share of positive assessments was comparable to Hungary, while the share of negative evaluations reached two-thirds.

However, for the purposes of the present study, it is more relevant how respondents evaluated the living conditions (standard of living) of their families. This is shown in the following Table 3.1.

The table shows that the respondents in Poland and Czechia evaluated their living standard positively more often than negatively, while the Polish expressed positive opinions even more frequently (in 41% of cases) than the Czechs (36% of respondents). In Slovakia, negative evaluation (26%) was slightly more frequent than a positive one (23%), and there was a decisively highest share of the neutral assessment "Neither good nor bad". The least positive view of living conditions in households was held by Hungarians, among whom only 13% provided positive answers, while 39% of respondents selected a negative answer.

When the respondents expressed their views on their future situation in this regard, the answers were overwhelmingly negative, except for Poland, where the share of positive and negative answers was identical, and 67% (the biggest share out of all surveyed countries) did not expect any changes, which can be perceived as a de facto positive view, given the relatively favourable current circumstances. Unflatteringly for the Czech Republic, its respondents were the most sceptical ones. Almost 40%

Table 3.2 The main income of the family

The main income of our family is						
	Czechia	Latvia	Germany	Poland	Slovakia	Ukraine
Income from employment	96.5	86.6	82.4	96	88.5	91.1
Income from social welfare	2.1	7	10.3	1.6	5	3
Other income	1.4	6.5	7.4	2.4	5	5.9
Sum	100	100.1	100.1	100	98.5	100

(the most out of all surveyed countries) expected a decrease in the quality of living conditions, while only 10% (the least out of all countries) were optimistic regarding the future in this area.

The following part presents the results of this research in comparison to other included countries. The first question concerned *the main family income*. The distinct categories of income from employment, income from welfare, and other income were established. The following Table 3.2 provides the results.

The table shows that extra employment income primarily concerned Germany, where more than 10% of families stated they are dependent on welfare, and more than 7% of families declared another form of income. In Latvia, the situation was similar (more than 13% in total). In this respect, the best situation is in the Czech Republic and Poland, where it only concerns roughly 4% of families. Clearly, there is some correspondence with the level of unemployment.

The following question in the survey enquired about *the experience of unemployment* in a family (in case of one of its members). Accordingly, this data is not necessarily related directly to the previous figures, since they examined the experience of unemployment, which might have taken place many years ago. The following Table 3.3 provides a full overview.

It is apparent that the greatest share of respondents who never experienced unemployment was found in Slovakia, followed by Latvia. In the remaining countries, the situation was similar and the share included about a half of the population.

Households' economic situation is further clarified by the provided data about the responses to the question *whether a family receives any governmental social support or welfare* (Table 3.4).

Table 3.3 Experience with family unemployment

I have experience with unemployment						
	Czechia	Latvia	Germany	Poland	Slovakia	Ukraine
Yes	47.5	55.9	48.1	48.4	62.6	46.6
No	52.5	44.1	51.9	51.6	37.4	53.4
Total	100	100	100	100	100	100

Table 3.4 Governmental social support or welfare for a family

As a family, we are receiving social welfare of some sort

	Czechia	Latvia	Germany	Poland	Slovakia	Ukraine
Yes	16.8	26.3	19.7	5.6	26.7	16.4
No	83.2	73.7	80.3	94.4	73.3	83.6
Total	100	100	100	100	100	100

Once again, the greatest percentage of positive answers was provided in Slovakia and Latvia (i.e. this is related to the aforementioned experience of unemployment), and to a lesser extent, in Germany. However, this question also covers receiving any kind of welfare (including parental allowance, etc.) by the family, which supplements its income. It is possible to assume this is related to welfare systems of individual countries. In such a case, the most complex situation is in Poland, where only 5.6% of families declared the entitlement to some sort of social welfare.

Other questions examined what the largest expenses in household are associated with (it was possible to give more answers). We tried to process all responses using the coding method, in the sense of examining, comparing and categorizing responses to an open question. On the basis of a repeated examination of the material, typical responses were identified, and the remaining ones were divided into prepared categories (types) on the basis of semantic similarity. Following this, the frequency of occurrence of individual types of answers was recorded statistically.

In total, nine types of answers regarding the largest expenses in a household were established. These were: housing, transportation, food, personal consumption, travel, education, spare time activities, savings, loans. However, some of them appeared insignificant in comparison to others due to their occurrence, namely travel, which was mentioned by 2–7% of respondents (most often in Germany—7.1%), expenses related to spare time activities (2–6%), savings/insurance and paying back loans, which, rather logically, did not constitute a significant expense item for a huge majority and it was given by 2–5% of households.

Transportation expenses are worth mentioning separately. While in general, they do not rank among critical expense items, there are rather big differences between surveyed countries. In Ukraine, Latvia and Slovakia, this expense item was only given by roughly 10%; however, in Poland and Czechia, it was ca 18%, and in Germany, it was important for 21.4% of families. By far the most frequently, housing was mentioned as the most expensive area (see the following Table 3.5).

Most frequently, this was the case in Czech and German households, as it was indicated by over 80% of respondents. In these countries, housing is the most expensive. They were followed by Slovakia, then by Latvia and Poland with some distance, and finally, in Ukraine, this item only concerned just under 25% of respondents.

Food costs constituted the second-largest item. The situation is illustrated by the following Table 3.6.

Table 3.5 Housing as the most expensive item

In our family, HOUSING constitutes the greatest expense item

	Czechia	Latvia	Germany	Poland	Slovakia	Ukraine
Yes	81	51.3	80.4	46.6	75.5	24.1
No	19	48.7	19.6	53.4	24.5	75.9
Total	100	100	100	100	100	100

Table 3.6 Food as the most expensive item

In our family, FOOD constitutes the greatest expense item

	Czechia	Latvia	Germany	Poland	Slovakia	Ukraine
Yes	67.8	58.4	23.2	30.5	75.5	17.9
No	32.2	41.6	76.8	69.5	24.5	82.1
Total	100	100	100	100	100	100

Food was the greatest expense item for the respondents in Slovakia and Czechia, which suggests there were the most expensive groceries. In Latvia, this item was considered crucial by a smaller percentage, with an even smaller percentage in Poland. In Germany and especially Ukraine, these expenses only appeared essential for less than one-quarter or one-fifth of families, respectively. Possibly, this was related not only to the cost of groceries, but also to the consumption of food in individual households.

This study also examined family expenses related to education in individual countries. They are shown in the following Table 3.7.

The provided table shows this item was primarily considered important in Ukraine and Latvia, followed by Slovakia. The data for the remaining countries is similar, with the least share of families who stated education-related expenses were important in Poland. These expenses are undoubtedly related to whether education is free in a given country, how many private schools are there, whether there is a tuition fee and at which schools, etc. Of course, the data was also influenced by the number of children attending higher education, which is associated with higher financial demands.

The socioeconomic situation of households can also be judged by *whether a family is able to save some earned money,* i.e. if it is able to generate a financial reserve (Table 3.8).

Table 3.7 Education as the most expensive item

In our family, EDUCATION constitutes the greatest expense item

	Czechia	Latvia	Germany	Poland	Slovakia	Ukraine
Yes	9.4	22.6	8.9	5.9	19.9	29
No	90.6	77.4	91.1	94.1	80.1	71
Total	100	100	100	100	100	100

Table 3.8 Ability to generate a financial reserve

We are able to save some of our monthly income

	Czechia	Latvia	Germany	Poland	Slovakia	Ukraine
Yes	60.9	30.1	51.3	44	54.4	72.6
No	39.1	69.9	48.7	56	45.6	27.4
Total	100	100	100	100	100	100

In this respect, the most problematic situation existed in Latvia, where only under a third of households was able to save some of their income. In Poland, it was a little over 40%. In other countries (Czechia, Slovakia, Germany), there was a similar share, specifically over a half of families. Interestingly, Ukraine had the highest share of such families. There may be two explanations for these differences. Firstly, it is certainly related to income (whether the family has anything left); secondly, it is important how much one plans for the future. The resulting figures are more or less in line with some other studies, which, e.g. show that in Czechia, for two-thirds of respondents who state they able to save some money, the respective amount does not exceed 1000 CZK.

From the perspective of socioeconomic evaluation, an *assessment of a general standard of living* was crucial. The opinions of respondents from individual countries are shown in the following Table 3.9.

It is apparent the best situation is in Germany (as it was to be expected), where 47.5% of households consider their standard of living as rather good or very good and only 10.3% as rather bad or very bad. In contrast, the greatest share of families who considered their living standard bad appeared in Latvia (19.6%). In other countries, the percentage of negative assessments was similar to one another. In the number of positive evaluations, Germany was followed, with some distance, by Poland (34.9%), Czechia (31.8%) and Ukraine (31.1%). The smallest amount of household reporting a rather good or very good standard of living was in Slovakia and Latvia.

Here, however, it should be noted there is a large variance in this assessment. The two countries mentioned last, together with Ukraine, clearly included the most people who considered their situation average. Overall, the distribution of households in

Table 3.9 Evaluation of a living standard in families

Overall, I rate our standard of living

	Czechia	Latvia	Germany	Poland	Slovakia	Ukraine
Very bad	1.7	3.8	2.6	0	1.4	0.5
Rather bad	9.8	15.9	7.7	10.3	8.4	7.2
Average	56.7	63.6	42.2	54.8	67.2	61.2
Rather good	26.7	15.9	38.5	32.5	19.5	26.3
Very good	5.1	0.8	9	2.4	3.5	4.8
Total	100	100	100	100	100	100

these countries indicates the lowest differentiation (towards poverty in Latvia, while in Ukraine, on the hand, the share of people considering their situation rather bad or very bad was the lowest out of all included countries). Clearly, German households manifested the greatest differentiation, as there was the smallest number of families considering their situation average, and the scissors of inequality were most open there, with almost a half of the families assessing their situation as rather good or very good, as already mentioned.

3.2 Satisfaction in Family Life

Life satisfaction is a topic that has recently been examined by a growing number of researchers from various fields. Furthermore, the interest in this issue has been growing in the past years. This has been thought to stem from a certain departure from both problems of adaptation and survival, and from purely material values. Some role has likely also been played by the growing individualism, which has due to its inherent focus on an individual led to a development of knowledge regarding individual well-being and, in relation to this, to an increased emphasis on an improvement of individual quality of life (Marklová 2007; Křivohlavý 2001). A search for a clear definition of the term "life satisfaction" has proved highly difficult. Frequently, the concepts like life satisfaction, subjective well-being and quality of life have been confused. However, there is an agreement that cognitive (evaluative) and affective components of all areas of life (e.g. health, psychological stability, social relations, etc.) can contribute to life satisfaction (Fahrenberg et al. 2001).

E. Diener, who invented one of the most widely used scales measuring life satisfaction (Diener et al. 1985), considers the notion of life satisfaction one of the components of subjective well-being. Besides life satisfaction, which he considers a cognitive (evaluative) constituent of subjective well-being, Diener also includes pleasant emotions as another component.

W. Wilson was one of the first authors who focused on individual well-being and life satisfaction, and he published its correlates already in 1967. According to him, a happy and satisfied person is young, rich, well-educated, well-paid, extroverted, optimistic, free of significant worries, religious and married. Furthermore, such people have great confidence in themselves, a good work ethic and adequate aspirations. There is no proved connection of satisfaction to gender or to a level of mental abilities (Marklová 2007).

However, in the past four decades, there has been a remarkable increase in the volume of research dedicated to identifying and better describing factors that influence life satisfaction and subjective well-being. Binarová (2008) describes four factors that have been proved in various studies: (1) demographic factors—income, age, gender, marriage and family; (2) behavioural factors—social contact, activities, life events; (3) personality factors—self-respect, temperament, intelligence; (4) biological factors (health).

As for demographic factors, there has been proved a two-way connection between marriage and life satisfaction. This means that happy and content people have a higher probability of entering marriage. According to numerous authors (Rybářová 2009), however, life with a partner or in marriage only has a positive correlation to individual well-being only if both partners are happy with the relationship. If they are not happy, the degree of subjective wellbeing rather tends to decrease. Regarding age, older papers argue repeatedly that young people are happier than old ones. Recently, however, some evidence has surfaced showing that age does not influence life satisfaction, or that there is in fact a positive correlation between age and satisfaction (Binarová 2008).

Personality is one of the strongest determinants of satisfaction with life. It has been proved that satisfaction with oneself showed the highest correlation with life satisfaction out of all possible variables. Interestingly, it has also been discovered that self-respect tends to decrease in unhappy people (Binarová 2008).

Regarding biological factors, it is widely assumed that health functions as an important determinant. While subjective health shows a high correlation, the correlation of objective health and life satisfaction is rather low (Diener et al. 2002). This might be explained by the fact that in referring to one's subjective health, a person also transmits his or her emotional state. Furthermore, the effect of health is dependent on the individual perception of a situation. In case of serious medical issues, the decrease in satisfaction follows due to the impossibility to fulfil important goals. However, if a disease is not serious, the person adapts and the satisfaction may remain unchanged.

Approaches focused on examining the abovementioned factors, which influence to a larger or smaller degree the level of life satisfaction, are mutually complementary. The experts have increasingly been expressing support for the hypothesis that different strategies work differently for different people. Thus, it is unnecessary to search for a universal cause of satisfaction. It is assumed that the correct solution is to focus on mutual interactions of the influence of culture, personality, aims and environment (Marklová 2007).

Despite some differences in definitions, most conceptions of life satisfaction, happiness and subjective well-being share the emphasis on the subjectivity of assessment—people are satisfied if they feel that way or if they say they feel that way. Subjective well-being is frequently perceived as an aspect of quality of life (Kebza and Šolcová 2003). The present paper also employs this notion of happiness and life satisfaction. Life satisfaction/happiness is considered a subjective category—people are happy and satisfied if they say they are.

In this respect, there are remarkable results available in the survey of Tuček, Kuchařová and other co-authors from the Institute of Sociology at the Czech Academy of Sciences (2001). The question *"What is important for happy family life?"* yielded the following responses (1496). The order of conditions for happy family life according to average rating (five-point scale: 5 = most important, 1 = least important):

Order—Average

1. Good medical condition of all family members 4.4
2. Permanent emotional relationship of partners 4.3
3. Faithfulness 4.2
4. Tolerance and appreciation 4.1
5. Possibility of having children 3.9
    ...
18. Division of household labour 3.2
19. Understanding regarding views on employment 3.1
20. Possibility of attending to one's own friends and interests 3.0
21. Agreement in opinions on public events 2.6
22. Same religious belief 2.2.

Most items from the list were considered important, but still, the views were differentiated. Average ratings had almost no connection to marital status. This means, e.g. that single people placed greater emphasis on the "possibility of attending to one's own friends and interests", divorced ones put lesser stress on "permanent emotional relationship of partners", but considered "tolerance" important, and married ascribed greater important to items related to children. The differences in mean among the noted subgroups were statistically significant; however, they only included several items; thus, there was not a significant shift in an overall perception on the requirements of happy marriage connected to marital status.

The degree of satisfaction as to the fulfilment of the abovementioned conditions of happy marriage was examined by the following question: "What are married people satisfied with?" The following overview shows the matters in family life people were most and least satisfied with (sorted according to average rating; five-point scale: 5 = most important, 1 = least important):

Order—Average

1. Possibility of having children 4.2
2. Faithfulness 3.9
3. Living separately from parents 3.9
4. Permanent emotional relationship with a partner 3.8
5. Sexual understanding 3.7
    ...
18. Opinions on public events 3.2
19. Possibility of attending to one's own friends and interests 3.1
20. Sufficient amount of money, good material conditions 3.1
21. Division of household labour 3.0
22. Overall climate in society 2.9.

Similarly, to the previous question regarding condition of happy family life, there was also a prevalent satisfaction with individual areas of family life. A differentiation of opinions only appeared in the category "most satisfied". 22% of respondents did not provide any area they were completely satisfied with (the grade 5). When the respondents reported the highest degree of satisfaction for 1–3 items, they most often included statements of facts ("I have children", "Good medical condition", "Separate living") as well as the quality of relationship ("Permanent emotional relationship", "Faithfulness", "Sexual understanding").

Regarding the representation of individual items, the situation was similar for negative answers (22% of respondents did not provide any items, more than 40% gave 1–3 items); however, it was necessary to merge the two lowest grades. When a respondent provided 1–3 items, the dissatisfaction was, besides the "climate in society", related to the evaluation of material conditions ("lack of money"). A great part of dissatisfaction was associated with the "possibility of attending to one's own friends and interests" and the "division of household labour".

The functioning of family is undoubtedly characterized by the division of roles. In the quoted survey, it was proved it is essential that the division of household labour is one of the areas people are least satisfied with. It is necessary to emphasize that for most people, the division of household labour is not an important precondition of a happy marriage. In this relation, it may be noted that women tend to be less satisfied with their lives. Coping with both job and family obligations often impacts negatively the regeneration of their own vitality. While they may have dealt with this eventually, it influences their dissatisfaction.

The present paper also examined what is important for satisfaction in family life, using simple questions. While this may seem a crude research tool at first glance, the results of discussions and long-term research show that even a simple question (or questions) can meaningfully record satisfaction, and the declared satisfaction with life can then be placed in relation to demographic and social factors (Hamplová 2004, 13).

There were two questions: "How do you imagine a happy family?" and "What would you need to be satisfied with your family life?" Given the question were again open, we followed the same course, i.e. we monitored the most frequent requirements for a happy family (it was possible to give more answers). We tried to process all answers using the method of coding; subsequently, we searched for typical answers and grouped all other items into prepared categories (types) according to similarity of content. Finally, the frequency of each type of answer was recorded statistically.

The following *factors of satisfaction* were established: health, good living conditions, material security, employment, option to spend spare time together, harmonious atmosphere in family (free of conflicts and stress), wholeness of family, successful and problem-free children.

Given the frequency of answers for individual established types, the present study focused primarily on the most common ones: harmonious atmosphere, relation in family, material/financial security and health. These factors ranked among the most frequent responses in all countries.

The greatest concordance occurred in case of the item *harmonious cohabitation free of conflict, general well-being*. This answer ranked most frequent in Ukraine and Germany was one of the most important factors in Slovakia; in the Czech Republic, it was somewhat less frequent, and the share was lowest in Poland (even there,

Table 3.10 Image of a happy family—emotional atmosphere

How do you imagine a happy family? HARMONIOUS RELATIONS, FREE OF ARGUMENTS AND CONFLICTS, EMOTIONAL ATMOSPHERE (FREE OF STRESS AND WORRIES; HAPPINESS, JOY, LIFE WELL-BEING, FRIENDSHIP)

	Czechia	Latvia	Germany	Poland	Slovakia	Ukraine
Yes	36.5	30.6	43.8	24.3	45.9	36.5
No	63.5	69.4	56.3	75.7	54.1	63.5
Sum	100	100	100	100	100	100

however, it ranked second behind *health*). In responses to this question, there were comparatively smallest differences between individual counties. The following Table 3.10 shows the specific percentages:

Beyond doubt, *health* of family members was of great importance for satisfaction of a family. Here, however, there were manifest differences between individual countries. This aspect of satisfaction was most important in the Czech Republic, where, as in Poland, it was selected most frequently. It ranked second in Ukraine, third in Slovakia, and it was least prominent in Germany. It is difficult to explain why this factor was neglected in Germany and ranked behind the need to engage in spare time, holidays and shared interests together. It is possible that some respondents (across individual countries) considered this factor a necessary condition of satisfaction with life. The following Table 3.11 provides specific figures.

The most frequent factors also included *material and financial security*, the share was, however, highly differentiated. It was considered most important in Slovakia and placed second in Czechia. In Germany, Poland, Latvia and Ukraine, it only ranked second. The importance of this factor was certainly related to value systems: the lifestyle of families, the importance of material possessions, the degree of consumerism in family lifestyle. The resulting representation is shown in the following Table 3.12.

The representation of the aforementioned established factors was scarce and mostly did not exceed 10%. Employment was most frequently mentioned in Czechia and Slovakia (11.7% in both cases). Other factors worth noting were the aforementioned requirement for spending spare time together and shared interests which was stated in Germany in 34.4% of cases and appeared rather significant in the Czech Republic as well (22.7%). Furthermore, wholeness of family seemed relatively important for a happy life. In Poland, it was mentioned in 16.5% of cases,

Table 3.11 Image of a happy family—health

How do you imagine a happy family? HEALTH

	Czechia	Latvia	Germany	Poland	Slovakia	Ukraine
Yes	51.2	37.3	18.8	39.8	33.8	28.6
No	48.8	62.7	81.3	60.2	66.2	71.4
Sum	100	100	100	100	100	100

Table 3.12 Image of a happy family—material and financial security

How do you imagine a happy family? MATERIAL AND FINANCIAL SECURITY, FINANCIAL AND SOCIAL BACKGROUND WITHOUT DEBTS AND MORTGAGES

	Czechia	Latvia	Germany	Poland	Slovakia	Ukraine
Yes	43.4	24.6	28.1	22.3	58.6	19
No	56.6	75.4	71.9	77.7	41.4	81
Sum	100	100	100	100	100	100

in Ukraine in 15.9% of cases, in Germany in 12.5% of cases, and in Czechia and Slovakia in 8.9% of cases.

In summary, it is possible to say the present results correspond to the above-mentioned survey, where medical condition and relations (tolerance, faithfulness) in family also ranked among the most important factors. In the 12 years since that survey, there has been a large shift in the important of material and financial security. This is probably related to an increased prominence of consumerist lifestyle and to the growing differentiation of society.

In responses to the question "What would you need to be satisfied?", *material and financial security* was again prevalent, together with time to spend some moments with family. In both cases, there were some differences. The following Table 3.13 summarizes answers with regard to material and financial satisfaction.

The table shows this aspect is most problematic in Slovakia and the Czech Republic. This is followed by Germany and Ukraine, but the differences between the remaining countries are negligible. This distribution essentially mimics the answers regarding the most important factor of family happiness (see the previous table). It appears this is caused by a huge focus on consumerist lifestyle, because of which material and financial security is considered essential in these countries. The results probably do not stem from generally worse material conditions.

As for the *lack of time to spend with family*, the results were again not distributed evenly (see the following Table 3.14).

Among the respondents, the Germans felt most often (in more than 50% of cases) they needed more time to spend with their families; thus, this factor appears crucial. This showed an effort and interest to achieve greater cohesiveness and improve the functioning of families. The Czech Republic and Poland followed with some

Table 3.13 Material and financial needs to be satisfied with a family life

What would you need to be satisfied with your family life? MATERIAL AND FINANCIAL SECURITY, FINANCIAL RESERVES FOR RETIREMENT

	Czechia	Latvia	Germany	Poland	Slovakia	Ukraine
Yes	37.4	23.8	28.6	20.5	40.7	26.9
No	62.6	76.2	71.4	79.5	59.3	73.1
Sum	100	100	100	100	100	100

Table 3.14 Time spent together as a need to be satisfied with a family life

What would you need to be satisfied with your family life? MORE TIME, SPARE TIME
SPENT TOGETHER (HOBBIES, INTERESTS, MORE HOLIDAYS, CULTURE …)

	Czechia	Latvia	Germany	Poland	Slovakia	Ukraine
Yes	25.2	21.7	55.1	30.7	19.8	19.2
No	74.8	78.3	44.9	69.3	80.2	80.8
Sum	100	100	100	100	100	100

distance. According to some studies, men are more sensitive to a lack of spare time, which consequently impacts family relations and increases the number of conflicts.

As for the remaining factors, no large percentage was recorded, except for wholeness of family in Poland, where 20.5% of families felt they needed it to be satisfied. It appears families in Poland are more sensitive to splits. Harmonious relations were most often lacking in Slovak families (15.7%).

The present chapter concludes with results from cases when respondents stated they did not miss anything to be satisfied. The greatest share of positive answers was recorded in Ukraine (31.4%) and Poland (26.9%). Interestingly, the smallest share of such answers was collected in Germany, where only 12.2% of families stated they did not need anything else to be satisfied. This can certainly be related to the requirements and specifics we demand in a "happy family". Overall, it has to be noted that the presented results have to be considered in the context of culture and comprehensive social and economic conditions in a given society.

References

Binarová, M. (2008). *Životní spokojenost a fungování rodin s tělesně postiženým dítětem.* Brno: Masarykova univerzita. Accessed 6 May 2017.

Červenka, J. (2013). Hodnocení ekonomické situace a materiálních životních podmínek v středoevropském srovnání. *Naše společnost,* CVVM SÚ ČAV. https://cvvm.soc.cas.cz. Accessed 21 June 2018.

Diener, E., Emmons, R. A., Larsen, R. J., & Griffin, S. (1985). The satisfaction with lifes scale. *Journal of Personality Assessmment, 49,* 71–75.

Diener, E., Lucas, R. E., & Oishi, S. (2002). Subjective well-being. In C. S. Snyder, & S. J. Lopez, (Eds.), *Handbook of positive psychology* (pp. 63–73). Oxford: Oxford University Press.

Fahrenberg, J., Myrtek, M., Schumacher, J., & Brähler, E. (2001). *Dotazník životní spokojenosti.* Praha: Testcentrum.

Hamplová, D. (2004). *Životní spokojenost: rodina, práce a další faktory.* Praha: Portál.

Kebza, V., & Šolcová, I. (2003). Well-being jako psychologick' a zároveň mezioborově založen' pojem. *Československá psychologie, 47*(4), 333–345

Kraus, B., et al. (2015). *Životní styl současné české rodiny.* Hradec Králové: Gaudeamus.

Křivohlavý, J. (2001). *Psychologie zdraví.* Praha: Portál.

Marklová, K. (2007). *Hodnoty jako předpoklad životní spokojenosti.* Brno: Masarykova univerzita.

Rybářová, A. (2009). *Životní události a životní spokojenost.* Brno: Masarykova univerzita.

Tuček, M., & Kuchařová, V. (2001). Proměny rodiny v období transformace. In.: Rodina – zdroj lidského kapitálu Evropy v 21. století. Sborník z česko-německo-rakouské konference. Brno: Národní centrum pro rodinu.

Chapter 4
Leisure Time in Family Life

Abstract The chapter in its first part presents changing understanding of leisure time in the past and currently. Major shifts have occurred in the increasing amount of free time and its democratization. The free time or leisure time is understood only just as a supplement or the rest after work; however, it has its intrinsic value, carries potential of freedom, self-realization, fun and relax. The text deals with leisure time functions and its meaning for individuals and complete family. It highlights issues that are connected with spending of leisure time. In the second part of the chapter, there are results of survey, which was mapping of family spending of free time, its amount and fulfilment. In all the surveyed countries, spending of leisure time has proved to be an important perquisite for family life satisfaction. Activities that are the most likely to be undertaken together with family members are watching TV, walks, trips, visits of friends or relatives, visits of cultural actions and social games.

Keywords Leisure time · Family life · Functions of leisure time · Leisure time activities · Lifestyle and leisure · Amount and quality of leisure

4.1 Meaning and Function of Leisure Time

Leisure time is part of a lifestyle and can significantly affect the quality of life. Balancing work with relaxation and changing diverse activities is important for maintaining a healthy lifestyle. The way you spend your free time is influenced by several factors and is specific to each person. In families, parents often determine the way of spending free time. Children can later take this model into their future independent lives. The way families spend their free time can also be an indicator of their social status. In recent decades, there have been changes in the area of leisure time in terms of its quantity and quality. The basic trend is an increase in leisure time as well as a wider range of various individual and group activities.

© The Author(s) 2020   65
B. Kraus et al., *Contemporary Family Lifestyles in Central and Western Europe*,
SpringerBriefs in Sociology, https://doi.org/10.1007/978-3-030-48299-2_4

4.1.1 Free Time in the History and Now

The alternation of activity and rest corresponds to the biorhythm of all living creatures; in case of man, it took a concrete form of alternation of work and leisure time. Leisure time has existed throughout the course of human history, but it has come to the forefront of interest gradually and slowly.

From the point of view of the development of leisure time, the nineteenth and twentieth centuries are particularly important. Attention to leisure time had an individual and collective dimension (Hofbauer 2010). Leisure time ceased to be a privilege of the nobility, since the beginning of the nineteenth century it has been promoted in the middle-class families, and in the second half of the nineteenth century also in the working-class families. Activities, associations and facilities opened itself up to new people from different social backgrounds, helping them to go beyond the traditional family framework.

The scientific character of leisure time studies was the origin of sociology of leisure time (Veselá 1999). **Thorstein Veblen** (1857–1929), an American of Norwegian origin, is considered to be its founder thanks to the book **The Theory of the Leisure Class** (1899). Veblen pointed out to the emergence of leisure time as a new important area of life, but at the same time he identified leisure time with idleness, and he criticized it. In addition to theoretical considerations, empirical studies began to emerge, the time-frame technique was improved, and factors influencing the leisure time structure of various population groups were identified. Leisure time was gaining in scope, importance and the interest of society in leisure time grew. Legislative documents of European countries as well as other emerging institutions dealt with it. Later, sciences on leisure time, e.g. leisure time education, came into being.

Most scientists had no doubt about the importance and value of leisure for individuals and society. They saw it from an individual point of view as a place for rest, fun, cultivation of abilities and skills; from the social point of view, time for the reproduction of the workforce, for the acquisition of culture and for the very cultural creation.

In the second half of the twentieth century, leisure time gained in scope, importance and aroused the interest of society.

A milestone in the study of leisure time was the 1962 book by French sociologist **Joffre Dumazedier entitled "Vers une civilization du loisir?" (Towards to a leisure time society?)**. It brought the idea that the main achievement of the modern civilization is not the material welfare, but the universality of the existence of leisure time, which affects all other spheres of life.

The title of the book is intentionally a question. The author wanted to draw attention to the ambivalence of leisure time. It can be a space for the positive development of an individual and for giving meaning to his place in society, but it can also lead to his isolation, to the lack of interest in what is going on outside of his privacy.

In the second half of the twentieth century, especially in the countries of Central and Eastern Europe, under the influence of the practice of the then Soviet Union, new concepts of education and leisure time association based on mass and unification were developed. Youth activities at the place of residence were supported. The participants were activated by working together with their peers.

The 1990s were a breakthrough period, and the consequences of globalization also began to show more significantly. The quantitative and qualitative development of leisure time activities of children and youth continued. At the same time, individualization in leisure activities developed. The differences in age, social and interest groups began to be considered. In this period, the influence of computers and modern technologies is beginning to grow significantly.

Němec et al. (2002) summarize the post-war development of the concept and content of leisure time into three stages:

1. **Stage—1950s and 1960s:**
   The lifestyle of society **favours work**, the opposite is free time. Therefore, rest and recreation become the basic function of leisure time in order to reproduce the workforce. In out-of-school education establishments, activities include rest, outdoor activities, walks and mass preparation for classes.
2. **Stage—1970s and 1980s:**
   There is **no longer a sharp differentiation between work and leisure time**. In our free time, we satisfy our material and cultural needs, free time serve not only for rest and recreation, but people also want entertainment and experiences. Numerous interest activities of all ages are developing.
3. **Stage—1990s:**
   From the balance between work and leisure time, we move towards **an excess of leisure time:**
   The borders between work, partly-leisure time and leisure time are blurred. People enter free time with the requirements of "I want", "I need", "I enjoy it", etc. Human cultivation is essential.

Summing up these changes in the understanding of leisure time, the increasing amount of leisure time and its democratization is essential.

In the first half of the nineteenth century, the average daily working hours in Europe were 12–14 h. Around 1900, a working week with 60 h of work prevailed. In the early 1930s, a requirement of 40 h of work per week was set across European countries. In 1978, working hours, counted into all days of the year, were 5.9 h per day in the USA, 6.4 h in England and 7.7 h in France (Hofbauer 2004).

Over the last two hundred years, the life span of the people in Europe has increased by half. While in 1800 the average life expectancy was about 50 years, at present the average life expectancy of the population in the European Union is almost 74 years (Czech Statistical Office 2018). The composition of life also changed significantly. H. W. Opaschowski (in Hofbauer 2004) gave an overview of the evolution of lifetime. He structured lifetime into three categories—(1) time devoted to biological needs (e.g. sleep, food), (2) time devoted to work, profession and (3) time which is freely available to man (i.e. free time). While at the beginning of the nineteenth century the structure of time (in the order of categories as given, respectively, and in percentages) was 41-34-25, at the beginning of the twenty-first century, the proportion was quite different: 40-9-51. This comparison shows that there was a similar amount of time to meet biological needs. However, the proportion of working and free time has fundamentally changed. Today, free time with its range occupies the first place in the structure of human life. The sphere of work gets to the last place.

Leisure time has been democratized over the past centuries, providing new opportunities for free decision-making. Nevertheless, paradoxes can be found in its development. During the nineteenth and twentieth centuries, efforts were made to reduce the amount of working time. However, some people are currently trying to expand their working hours. They work overtime, refuse to take a holiday and look for second jobs. Some European countries are considering raising working hours again, and retirement age is also raising up. The reason and motive of these measures is probably an increase in the efficiency of the economy, an effort to maintain the standard of living of the society and a reaction to current demographic trends.

Despite these paradoxes, the development of leisure time can be described as positive from the family perspective. By reducing the long working hours of parents, more favourable conditions for family life and raising children were created. The wage labour of children and youth has been eliminated. Leisure time has become an important part of life. On the one hand, it contains perspectives and opportunities, and on the other hand, it also contains difficulties and risks.

In the following text, we will look at the ways in which leisure time is currently perceived and defined in more detail.

4.1.2   What is Leisure Time?

There are many definitions of leisure time in pedagogy, sociology, psychology and other disciplines. The simplest division of time is given by Kolesárová (2016) and divides time into two basic categories—**working and non-working time**. Non-working time (i.e. time after work) is further divided into **free and bound time**. In the bound time can be included activities that are necessary, and people do not do them out of interest or free will (e.g. ensuring the running of the household, transport to work).

Kaplánek (2012) points out at the fact that when defining leisure time, we distinguish between leisure time in a broader sense and leisure time in a narrower sense. Leisure time in the broader sense includes all time outside of working hours. Free time in the strict sense of the term contains only activities that one devotes to himself/herself entirely to his/her own free choice.

Structured time is more detailed in Vážanský (2001) and lists the following categories:

1. **working time**
2. **bound time**—time related to work (e.g. commuting, compulsory education after work)
3. **non-working time**—this is further divided by:

(a) **time for personal provision** (sleep, nutrition, hygiene, supply),
(b) **time for roles of necessity** (family and social commitments),
(c) **individually available time**—can be divided into
   (i) **partly-leisure time**—activities that the individual carries out partly as a hobby and partly as a duty, e.g. handwork, gardening, work in home workshop
   (ii) **leisure time**—time for yourself and your interests.

The perception and definition of "leisure time" is varied. The term "leisure time" can be understood either neutrally—time that is not yet fulfilled by anything, positively—free time, or negatively—unfulfilled, wasted time (Kaplánek 2012).

Knotová (2011) has a similar view on leisure time. She presents different concepts of leisure time—optimistic and sceptical. Knotová presents the concept of optimistic leisure time as meaningful. Sceptical approach, on the other hand, highlights the potential risks and negative aspects of leisure time.

Perception of leisure time is influenced by subjective view. It always depends on the individual, his/her value orientation and lifestyle. Some people consider leisure time to be a waste of time, for others it has a higher value in relation to the development of their personality, or it can be a period of rest after work. The same activity (e.g. plant cultivation) is for one person working time, for another purely leisure time, for others it falls into the category of partly-leisure time.

A similarly diverse situation is in the search for a definition of leisure time. There are usually two different definitions of leisure time in the literature—negative and positive (e.g. Vážanský 2001; Hofbauer 2004; Kaplánek 2012, 2017; Kolesárová 2016; Kraus et al. 2015):

1. **Quantitative, negative definition of leisure time**—defines leisure time by what it does not contain, what is not leisure time. It is a traditional and historically older approach, in literature, that appeared especially in the 1960s and 1970s. It is based on the definition of free time in relation to working hours. It defines it as a residual time that remains after deducting working time, completing given tasks and meeting basic needs. This is the approach of the French sociologist and founder of leisure time pedagogy, Joffre Dumazedier, who does not include into leisure time:

   • time spent on employment for adults, and in case of adolescents' time devoted to learning;
   • time devoted to preparation and transport to work or school;
   • time needed to meet basic biological needs (sleep, food, hygiene and other self-service activities);
   • the time needed to fulfil other duties (e.g. related to households).

Thus, leisure time is a set of activities that a person does for his/her own pleasure, either to relax or to have fun, or to develop their awareness, personality, voluntary social participation or free creative ability after fulfilling work, family and social responsibilities and obligations (Dumazedier 1966).

2. **Qualitative, positive definition of leisure time**—defines leisure time on the basis of its quality and focuses on the content of leisure time. It is a time that a person can freely dispose; it means a true freedom for an individual.

   In the negative definition of leisure time, we can see that duties (work, family, satisfying physiological needs) are given first, and time that is disposable is given the second place. The positive definition of leisure time refers mainly to freedom, interests, self-realization, recreation and entertainment.

Nowadays, experts incline to the second concept. *"Leisure time is a time in which one freely chooses and does such activities that bring joy, pleasure, enjoyment, relaxation, which restore and develop his physical and mental abilities and eventually creative skills as well. It is the time in which man is him/her-self, and mostly belongs to him/her-self, when he/she performs mostly freely and voluntarily activities for himself or herself. Eventually for others, out of their inner impulse and interest.* (Němec et al. 2002, p. 17).

Kratochvílová (2004) defines leisure time as a time of freedom that the individual has at his or her own disposal beyond his/her duty of self-expression and self-realization according to his/her own needs and interests. She states that everyone should be free to decide how to use their free time.

The aspect of freedom in leisure time is also evident in legislation. The Universal Declaration of Human Rights mentions the right to leisure time. Article 27 reads as follows:

> (1) Everyone has the right freely to participate in the cultural life of the community, to enjoy the arts and to share in scientific advancement and its benefits. (2) Everyone has the right to the protection of the moral and material interests resulting from any scientific, literary or artistic production of which he is the author. (https://www.un.org/en/universal-declaration-human-rights/)

In response to the Universal Declaration of Human Rights, the World Leisure Board of Directors approved The Charter for Leisure in the year 2000 (The World Leisure Organization 2001).

The right to leisure time is also included in the Convention on the Rights of the Child (1989). Article 31 of the Convention states that states parties recognize the right of the child to rest and to leisure time, to participate in play and recreational activities appropriate to his or her age, and to freely participate in cultural life and artistic activities; they help to provide children with adequate and equal opportunities in cultural, artistic, rest time and leisure activities (https://www.unicef.org/child-rights-convention/convention-text).

These approaches imply that the value of leisure time is both individual and social. From an individual point of view, it consists in creating space for self-realization and human development. The value in terms of society is because it can be used rationally for its benefits. From the individual's point of view, it is possible to define basic **functions of leisure time**: relaxation, cultivation, personality development (Kolesárová 2016). The functions are similarly described by Kraus et al. (2015). He sets among the three basic functions of leisure time the function of **relaxation** (relaxation, regeneration), **entertainment** (compensation) and **cultivation** (personality development). The function of **socialization** (socialization, belonging to a group) is also characteristic for youth.

Leisure time pedagogues often rely on the description of leisure time functions created by the important German leisure time pedagogue Horst W. Opaschowski (In: Vážanský 2001). He based definitions of the functions of leisure time on individual needs of the individual and current social requirements at the end of the twentieth century:

- **the need for recreation**—recovery, relief from daily stress, rest, activities beneficial to health;
- **need for compensation**—balancing deficiencies, distractions, promoting nature, conscious use of life, eliminating disappointment, frustration;
- **need for education**—knowledge, education, desire for experiences;
- **the need for contemplation**—peace, well-being, contemplation, time for oneself, seeking the meaning of life, finding identity;
- **need for communication**—communication, contacts, sociability, searching for social relations, desire to share common experiences;
- **the need for integration**—grouping, social security and stability, a sense of belonging, seeking emotional security, adherence to rituals and traditions;
- **the need for participation**—engagement, initiative, participation in social life and shaping the environment through social activities;
- **need for enculturation**—creative development, participation in cultural life, creative application.

These needs could be divided into individual needs (recreation, compensation, education, contemplation) and general needs, respectively social (communication, integration, participation, enculturation). All needs are reflected in functions of leisure time. These intertwine with each other, and the need to analyse leisure time activities comprehensively in the family, school, the media or a village is becoming increasingly important. The functions and goals of leisure time activities, contents, methodology and material facilities have substantially expanded in recent decades.

4.1.3 Leisure Time and Family

A family, as a primary social group, is also a prime environment of leisure time and upbringing for children and young people. The ways in which leisure time activities are carried out in families vary depending on their social status, lifestyle and relation to leisure time needs. A desirable goal is the interest of the family in enabling children to spend their free time actively, meaningfully, on the basis of their voluntary decision. At the same time, sensitive leading by parents or other members of the family is important. The family should inspire, support and implement children's leisure time activities, approach them in a creative way and create attitudes that children will be able and willing to apply in the future even after their own family is established.

Bendl et al. (2015) point out at the fact that family activities differentiate in some ways from the influence of school and school institutes. It is not possible to expect a professional approach from parents because they usually do not have a pedagogical education, but there are strong emotional relationships between its members. The quality of these relationships is essential for the educational effect of the family.

This action takes place:

1. **Reproduction of similar patterns of positive leisure time behaviour of parents**. Parents should be able to manage their free time appropriately, not overestimate it or underestimate it. It should be evident from the behaviour of parents that both the fulfilment of duties and leisure time are a natural part of our lives, that leisure time activities include, besides rest and relaxation, personal interests, our hobbies. It is desirable that children encounter the mutual tolerance of their parents to the interests of their partner, that they see some interests in common.

   Significant influence of parents as role models is confirmed by the results of a research from 2009, which was attended by Czech children aged 9–17. The most common answer to the question: "To whom do you want to resemble in adulthood?" Was the "someone from the family" option, which was answered by 40% of children (Stašová et al. 2015). However, the imitation of the lifestyle of parents is desirable only if there is no anti-social activity or that boredom does not prevail.

2. **Experiencing the free time together**, carrying out individual and common regular leisure time activities within the family (sports, tourism, art, science, technology, entertainment, etc.). However, activities need to be chosen in which all members can participate and feel comfortable. The nature of each activity must be appropriate to the age of all family members, their capabilities and interests.

3. **Promoting children's interests**, responsive and purposeful responses to needs, interests and talents of children. It is essential to listen to own children, to show real interest and to show them the joy from their success. Parents' participation in presenting the results of their children's hobbies, material support, accompanying hobbies or transport is essential. In particular, it is essential to respect the fact that leisure time activities are voluntary. It is beneficial to define each time together with children a specific goal towards which children will aim (Hofbauer 2004; Bendl 2015).

An important starting point is enough time devoted to children by parents and active, educated interest of parents.

In each family, leisure time is shaped by various factors, such as family size and type, living conditions of the family, whether the family is complete or one of the parents is missing, the family's economic security, housing standards, the family's social status, the way the family organizes free time, attitudes and values of parents. The number of children and their sex, the age of parents and children and the style of education also play a role. Interests of parents and their mutual tolerance are also very important.

A number of factors complicate the quality of the way we fill in the leisure time. For example, there are disproportions in the amount of free time. There are some individuals or groups who have a lot or very little of free time.

In the case of lack of leisure time, it is mainly because of work/school duties overload, a large number of leisure time activities or pursuing only one, narrowly focused leisure time activity, or time requirements for commuting to work.

Němec et al. (2002) draw attention to the fact that some individuals and whole families approach leisure time consumedly. The meaning of life becomes for them to gain as much money and material well-being as possible. Instead of taking advantage of the gradual shortening of working hours for own development, they become slaves to their own needs; devotes the time to the second job with the prospect of profit more money, respectively, gaining higher social prestige. In this way, the free time, which brings joy, relaxation, freedom, disappears from life.

On the other hand, there are individuals with a lot of free time, could be said with an abundance of free time, but they are not able to use it appropriately. This problem concerns, e.g. unemployed people. They have enough time, but usually lack the resources to spend their free time in their interests or motivation.

Nowadays, it is also possible to record the problematic ratio between active and passive forms of the use of leisure time. Especially among the young generation, mass media activities have been preferred over the last decades (Sak and Saková 2004; Kraus et al. 2015). These are passive activities, sometimes even harmful to the physical, mental and social development of the young generation. Other problems also include the relationship between the desire to pursue a particular activity during the leisure time and its actual implementation. According to Sak (2000), self-study during leisure time among the youth decreased as well as reading and active movement, interest in public or political activity have declined in the past ten years as well. On the other hand, they spend more time talking to peers (currently mainly in social networks), visiting restaurants and gainful employment. The most common reasons that prevent the pursuit of leisure time activities according to wishes and interests are mainly lack of time, money, unavailability of suitable opportunities in the surrounding area or poor equipment for running the selected leisure time activity.

The leisure time activities reflect the influences and consequences of the society's development. There are quantitative and qualitative changes in leisure time. On one hand, the possibilities for applying new approaches (animation, experiential education) are being expanded and new institutions are created to respond to specific needs, but on the other hand, leisure time is also a space of various pitfalls and dangers (allowing doing nothing, boredom, and in extreme cases undesirable or risky behaviour). As Hofbauer (2004) writes, the development of leisure time can therefore not be understood linearly as a "upward and forward" journey, but as a continuous uncovering of new possibilities, solutions to traditional and new issues.

4.2   Leisure Activities in Families in Terms of Quantity and Quality

In the lifestyle research of contemporary families in Europe, we first looked at how respondents perceived leisure time as a circumstance for a happy family. Parents who participated in the research were asked an open question: "How do you imagine a happy family?" Their responses were subject to content analysis, and nine categories were created: health, housing, employment, financial security, leisure time spent together, mutual help and support, harmonic relationships, success and satisfaction of children, complete family. The three most important areas that respondents associate with family satisfaction are health, mutual assistance and support and harmonious relationships. The category of leisure time spent together was ranked 3rd–6th in individual countries. It is considered as a significant item (3rd place) by the Germans (first and second place is support and assistance and harmonious relationships; 4th place in this country was financial security and health ranked fifth). In Poland and Ukraine, leisure time is ranked in sixth place.

Similarly, another open question was evaluated: What do you lack for your family's satisfaction?

In all countries included in the survey, the third place (ranked by frequency of responses) got the answer "I miss nothing, I am happy with my family". In Ukraine, it was even the most common answer chosen by 31% of respondents. In this country, the second place went to financial security, the third place took mutual assistance and support, and the fourth place was assigned to leisure time spent together. In other countries, lack of leisure time spent with the family was perceived as the first or second most common problem (it was similar with the category of financial security).

As is evident from the results of respondents' answers, leisure time is perceived as an important component of family satisfaction. The lack of common leisure time is perceived negatively and respondents have identified it as one of the two biggest obstacles to family satisfaction.

The following question tried to reveal in more detail the respondents' satisfaction with the quantity and quality of their leisure time. Respondents commented on eight items, choosing a level of satisfaction on a seven-point scale, where one extreme value was the option of "very satisfied" and the other "very dissatisfied". Between the extreme statements were the possibilities "dissatisfied, rather dissatisfied, neither dissatisfied nor satisfied, rather satisfied, satisfied. The results and country comparison are shown in Table 4.1. In the table, the range of options is narrowed down to "dissatisfied" (brings together "very dissatisfied, dissatisfied and rather dissatisfied"), "neither satisfied nor dissatisfied" and "satisfied" (brings together "rather satisfied, satisfied, very satisfied").

Satisfaction with the amount of their free time predominates among respondents from the Czech Republic and Latvia. In contrast, in Germany, Poland, Slovakia and Ukraine, there are more dissatisfied parents with the amount of their free time during working days (after work). In Poland, the highest percentage of those who chose the

Table 4.1 Satisfaction with the amount of free time after work (in %)

With the amount of leisure time after work I am:

	The Czech republic	Latvia	Germany	Poland	Slovakia	Ukraine
Dissatisfied	41.3	29.6	46	50	44.7	35.4
Neither satisfied nor dissatisfied	11.3	20.2	11.8	16.1	14.7	31.1
Satisfied	47.4	50.1	42.1	33.9	39.1	33.4

extreme option "very dissatisfied" is 10.5%. If we looked at the results for the whole sample of respondents, the same percentage of satisfied and dissatisfied came out, 41%. In the middle category of undecided, 17.5% of respondents are for the whole sample.

Table 4.2 shows respondents' satisfaction with the amount of their free time on weekends:

An analysis of the results in Table 4.2 shows that parents in most of the countries under review are significantly more satisfied with leisure time at the weekend in comparison to leisure time on weekdays. Only in Poland remains the prevailing dissatisfaction over satisfaction, 46% of respondents feel dissatisfied with the amount of free time on weekends. In the overall comparison for the whole sample, 24% of respondents are dissatisfied and 63% are satisfied.

The third item of the question concerned satisfaction with the length of leave. The results are shown in Table 4.3.

Note: In Europe, the length of legal leave varies, most often between 20 and 28 days per year. In some countries, the number of days of leave depends on the age

Table 4.2 Satisfaction with the amount of free time at the weekend (in %)

With the amount of free time on the weekend I am:

	The Czech Republic	Latvia	Germany	Poland	Slovakia	Ukraine
Dissatisfied	20	18.6	22.4	46	19.9	17.6
Neither satisfied nor dissatisfied	10.1	13.1	10.5	12.7	14.5	17.2
Satisfied	70	68.3	67.1	41.3	65.7	65.1

Table 4.3 Satisfaction with length of leave (in %)

With the length of leave I am:

	The Czech Republic	Latvia	Germany	Poland	Slovakia	Ukraine
Dissatisfied	26.7	18.8	38.7	44.4	34.1	32
Neither satisfied nor dissatisfied	11	13	14.7	14.5	13.9	13.6
Satisfied	62.4	68.2	46.7	41.1	48.8	54.4

of the worker or how long he goes to work. Employees with children, people with disabilities, or people under 18 years or workers before retirement are also favoured in some places (Hovorková 2018).

As in the previous table, satisfaction with the length of vacation prevails. Only in Poland are more dissatisfied respondents than satisfied. By contrast, respondents from Latvia are most satisfied with the length of their leave. In the overall comparison, 33% of the respondents are dissatisfied and 54% are satisfied. Thirteen percentage are neither satisfied nor dissatisfied.

Tables 4.1, 4.2 and 4.3 show that parents in the countries under review are most satisfied with the amount of free time on weekends, while they are the least satisfied with the amount of free time during normal working days.

The following two items examined respondents' satisfaction with the quality of rest. Table 4.4 reports satisfaction with the quality of rest during the holiday.

Table 4.4 shows that respondents' satisfaction with the quality of holiday rest is higher than satisfaction with the length of vacation. The greatest satisfaction was recorded by parents from the Czech Republic, the most dissatisfied can be found in Poland. Overall, 21% of respondents are dissatisfied, 64% satisfied and 15% chose the middle scale.

More generally, satisfaction with the quality of leisure time was measured, without closer time specification (Table 4.5).

The results in Table 4.5 are similar to the previous item. Quality of was rated the best by respondents from Latvia (almost 70%). There was a slight increase in undecided parents who chose the middle variant (a total of 20%). Overall, satisfaction is at 61%, dissatisfaction at 19%.

Table 4.4 Satisfaction with holiday rest quality (in %)

With the quality of the rest that holiday brings me, I am:	The Czech Republic	Latvia	Germany	Poland	Slovakia	Ukraine
Dissatisfied	12.7	17.8	25.3	29.9	22.3	19.4
Neither satisfied nor dissatisfied	10.7	15.7	17.3	9.7	12.6	23.8
Satisfied	76.5	66.6	57.4	60.5	65.2	56.9

Table 4.5 Satisfaction with quality of leisure time (in %)

With the quality of leisure that brings me free time, I am:	The Czech Republic	Latvia	Germany	Poland	Slovakia	Ukraine
Dissatisfied	18.2	12.7	17.1	21.4	23.7	21.8
Neither satisfied nor dissatisfied	13.7	17.5	26.3	17.5	17	25.2
Satisfied	68.2	69.7	56.6	61.1	59.4	52.9

Section 4.1 introduced leisure time, its understanding and structure. In addition to rest, leisure time can be filled with leisure time activities. Leisure time activities are focused on meeting and developing individual needs, interests and abilities. Unlike entertainment and relaxation, leisure time activities are always of an active nature (Němec et al. 2002). According to the content, hobbies can be divided into five areas: **social sciences** (e.g. learning foreign language, collecting, journalism, history, homeland studies), **technical–practical** (e.g. modelling, work with materials—paper, wood, glass, textiles; electronics, cooking), **natural science** (cultivation, breeding, protection of the nature, fishing, apiculture, hunting), **aesthetic education** (art, music, literature, drama), **sports and tourism** (fitness and health exercises, sports games, seasonal sports) (Pávková et al. 2002).

Leisure time activities are usually associated with the age category of children and youth, but leisure time activities are a source of self-realization, personal development and joy for adults as well. Table 4.6 shows how satisfied parents are with the amount of time to realize their interests.

The greatest satisfaction with the amount of time for their leisure time activities is felt by parents from Germany and Latvia. On the other hand, the greatest dissatisfaction was expressed by respondents from Slovakia, Ukraine and Poland. Overall, satisfaction prevails (51% of all respondents), in comparison to dissatisfaction (35%).

Leisure time includes, among other things, social activities, meeting family, friends. Research has shown (see above) that care for healthy relationships is a precondition for a happy family life for most respondents. Table 4.7 shows how satisfied parents are with the amount of time they spend with their loved ones.

The greatest satisfaction is found with parents in Germany (70%), the greatest dissatisfaction in Poland (41%). Compared to the previous table, there was a slight increase in overall satisfaction (55%) and a decrease in dissatisfaction (31%).

Table 4.6 Satisfaction with the amount of free time for leisure time activities (in %)

With the amount of free time on the weekend I am:	The Czech Republic	Latvia	Germany	Poland	Slovakia	Ukraine
Dissatisfied	39.4	21	21	42.1	42.5	42.3
Neither satisfied nor dissatisfied	14.5	14.2	13.2	15.1	11.1	15.4
Satisfied	46.1	64.9	65.8	42.9	44.9	42.3

Table 4.7 Satisfaction with the amount of free time devoted to close people (in %)

With the amount of time I can spend with my loved ones, I am:	The Czech Republic	Latvia	Germany	Poland	Slovakia	Ukraine
Dissatisfied	30.6	26	18.2	41.2	35.3	35.4
Neither satisfied nor dissatisfied	14.5	10.1	11.7	13.5	12.9	18.7
Satisfied	54.8	63.6	70.2	45.3	51	45.9

Table 4.8   Satisfaction with leisure time variety (in %)

With the variety of my free time, I am:

	The Czech Republic	Latvia	Germany	Poland	Slovakia	Ukraine
Dissatisfied	27.9	21.4	18.9	33.6	31.7	37.5
Neither satisfied nor dissatisfied	19.4	17.4	12.2	18.4	19.9	23.6
Satisfied	52.7	61.2	68.9	48	46.3	39

The last item of the question related to satisfaction with the variety of leisure time of respondents (Table 4.8).

Of the total number of respondents, 53% are satisfied with the variety of activities by which they fulfil their leisure time. The most satisfied parents are in Germany (almost 69%). On the contrary, the most dissatisfied respondents are in Ukraine. They are above average (29%) with 38% of dissatisfied respondents.

From all the tables above, it shows that among our respondents' satisfaction with both the quantity and quality of their free time usually prevails over dissatisfaction. In comparison of the countries, the most satisfied are the inhabitants of Latvia, followed by the inhabitants of the Czech Republic. The greatest dissatisfaction with leisure time can be seen at parents from Poland. The question is, to what extent an individual can change the circumstances that are often given to a country by its history. Limits for spending leisure time are set by the state's social policy, its economic level, the number of services provided and their quality, etc.

Several other questions focused on specific leisure time activities of families. The open question asked what respondents would like to do together in their free time as a family. In all countries, trips, travelling, common entertainment, social games and sports were the most common. In this question, respondents could also indicate what prevented them from carrying out these activities. There were two main reasons—lack of time and lack of finance.

Spending leisure time within the family can be divided into active and passive. Active spending of leisure time is activities in which family members participate directly, influence their process and outcome. The activities include board games, sports, hiking, cognitive activities, playing musical instruments and much more. Passive leisure time activities include mainly watching television, watching sport games, visiting the cinema, theatre and meeting friends. These are activities in which family members participate indirectly and cannot fully influence their process (Žumárová, In: Kraus et al. 2015).

The research included questions that try detect typical leisure activities today. An example of spending leisure time passively is playing computer games. In the young generation, computer-related activities become first in the frequency of leisure time activities in recent years (Kolesárová 2016). According to researches by Sak and Saková (2004) and Kolesarová (2016) in the category of 15–18-year-old Czech youth, there was a sharp increase in interest in computers from the mid-1990s to 2005. On the other hand, interest in watching television began to decline after 2000.

Since 2008, the number one and two in free time activities of Czech youth has a computer and chat with friends (nowadays often through social networks). The trend is similar in the 15–40 age group. The three most common leisure time activities are watching TV, chatting with friends and working with a computer.

The question in our research was: "Do you ever play computer games together at home?".

Gaming together is the most widespread in Poland (43% of Polish respondents) and Ukraine (32% of Ukrainian respondents). On the contrary, this activity is the least popular in Germany, where it occurs in only 1/4 families.

The active way of spending leisure time was addressed by the question: "Do you do sport in your free time?" Most respondents who do sport occurred in Germany (83% of German parents). The least sporting respondents were in Ukraine (43%) and Poland (48%). However, it should be taken into account that the choice of leisure time activities is determined, inter alia, by the way of livelihood, employment. If, in some countries, a larger proportion of the population is employed in positions requiring physical exertion, these people can be expected to spend their leisure time more by relaxing, passively. On the other hand, in countries where the majority of people are employed in services, their work is not physically demanding, they can be expected to prefer sports and physical activities in their free time.

The most frequently represented types of sport activities were: cycling, running, hiking, swimming, fitness. There are slight differences in preferences across countries. Cycling is the most popular sport activity in the Czech Republic and Germany. It has a second place in Poland and Slovakia, but in Ukraine it is only seventh. Skiing is the second most popular sport activity in the Czech Republic. On the contrary, in other countries, skiing ranked seventh or worse. The second most popular activity in Germany is various forms of health exercises (yoga, Pilates, bosu, etc.). In other countries, they were around tenth place. The third most frequently pursued sport activity in Germany is running. It is the most popular activity in Slovakia and the second most popular activity in Ukraine. Fitness activities (gym, aerobics, Zumba, etc.) are most often performed in Poland and Ukraine. Swimming is also popular in both countries.

Interesting results were provided by the question in which respondents were to define the amount of daily leisure time in hours. This is indicative, because the answers could have affected the respondents' subjective view of what to include in their leisure time and could have been inaccurate—each day is different, and it is difficult to find the average. For example, a time frame would provide more accurate data.

Table 4.9 shows how is it with the respondents and their amount of leisure time in each country. For comparison, the free time of men and women is given.

The question was also offered by the extreme option "I never have free time" or "I have free time only on holidays and weekends". In Latvia (11% of men and 8.2% of women) and in Germany (9.6% of men and 10% of women) were the most respondents who said that they have no free time. If we sum the two answers together,

Table 4.9 Amount of free time in hours (in %)

Amount of free time in hours

	The Czech Republic		Latvia		Germany		Poland		Slovakia		Ukraine	
	Men	Wo men	Men	Wo men	Men	Wo men	Men	Wo men	Men	Wo men	Men	Wo men
0 or just during the weekend	12.6	9.2	**33.3**	**30**	**28.8**	20	28.2	27.1	16.1	12.4	17.2	15
Max. 1 h	14.4	21.6	8	12.7	21.2	18.3	19.3	31.8	7.7	9.2	10	9.8
2–3	38.9	39.1	16.3	22.9	30.8	38.4	24.4	27.1	22.8	35.9	33.4	33.5
4–5	20.3	18.8	14	15.8	11.5	16.7	16.7	8.4	11.4	8.1	25	24.8
6 and more	6.5	7.8	5.3	6.2	3.8	0	7.7	3.7	**10.3**	8.2	**11.7**	**16**
In summary:												
0–1	27	30.8	41.3	42.7	**50**	38.3	**47.5**	**58.9**	23.8	21.6	27.2	24.8
2–3	38.9	39.1	16.3	22.9	30.8	38.4	24.4	27.1	22.8	35.9	33.4	33.5
4–6	**26.8**	26.6	19.3	22	15.3	16.7	24.4	12.1	21.7	16.3	**36.7**	**40.8**

Note: The numbers in bold are the most significant discussed in the text

in Latvia, 30% of women and 33.3% of men have almost no free time. In Germany, it is 28.8% of men, while German 20% of women. Poland is the third country where 28.2% of men and 27.1% of women said they have no free time at all or only on weekends.

The second extreme option was "I have 6 or more hours of free time a day". Most parents from Ukraine (16% women and 11.7% men) chose this option and then men from Slovakia (10.3%).

If we consider 2–3 h of free time per day as the mean and most frequently chosen values, we can summarize the number of respondents who have less (i.e. no free time or maximum 1 h per day) or more free time (i.e. 4 to 6 h' free time per day). The most significant deficit of leisure time is in Poland (58.9% female 47.5% male). Half of the German men also have no time or no more than 1 h a day. On the contrary, they are in the best position with a lot of free time in Ukraine. 40.8% of Ukrainian women and 36.7% of men have more than 4 h of free time per day. Parents from the Czech Republic are also doing well in this sense (26.8% men and 26.6% women).

Each family's lifestyle differs depending on the values and priorities of its members. Eight areas of life values were presented to the respondents, and they were asked to rank them according to priorities of their family. Number 1 was the most important priority. The index of the area was calculated on the basis of the order chosen (the lower the number, the more important it is). Table 4.10 provides an overview of the indexes for each country. The column for each country is divided into two sub-columns. The first shows the calculated index of priorities, and the second shows the ranking of the individual areas chosen by respondents from the given country (1–8).

Interestingly, respondents from all countries agreed on the first two priorities, but the rest is in different order. Health is the most important value in all countries. In the second place is happy family life. In Latvia and Germany, the third priority is a healthy environment, while in the Czech Republic and Slovakia, this area ended up seventh (penultimate). Good and interesting work is the third priority for the people of Poland. For Ukrainians, this is financial security. For the Czechs and Slovaks, the third important area is shared leisure time. In other countries, leisure time was ranked fifth. For the most of the countries, the last item was the work for other people, only in Poland the last area was the personal character and moral qualities.

In addition to the amount of free time, it is important to look at its content. Respondents were offered 16 areas of various leisure time activities, and they were allowed to choose a maximum of 5 areas typical for them. Table 4.11 gives an overview of how the activities are represented in each country. The numbers in the table indicate how many per cent of respondents in that country chose this activity.

Dominating activities are reading and watching TV. The order of activities varies from country to country.

In the Czech Republic, 60% of respondents are reading and watching TV in their free time. Trips and walks are third (56%), followed by gardening (51%). The same activities are also the most frequent in Latvia. Most respondents from this country watch TV (75%) in their free time, followed by reading (72%), gardening (70%), trips and walks (58%). All of these four activities are most prevalent in Latvia. In other

Table 4.10 Values and priority areas of family lifestyles

Important values and areas of lifestyle in individual countries														
	The Czech Republic		Latvia		Germany		Poland		Slovakia		Ukraine			
	Index	Ranking	Index	Ranking	Index	Ranking	Index	Ranking	Index	Ranking	Index	Ranking		
Good and interesting work	4.4	4	4.2	4-5	4.5	4	4.1	3	4.7	4	4.6	4		
Healthy and safe environment	5.9	7	4.0	3	4.3	3	5.0	4	5.5	7	5.4	6		
Happy family life	2.3	2	2.4	2	2.6	2	2.1	2	2.5	2	3.0	2		
Material level, financial sufficiency	5.8	6	5.7	6	6.0	7	5.5	6	5.4	6	4.5	3		
Health	**1.45**	1	**2**	1	**2.55**	1	**1.9**	1	**1.5**	1	**1.9**	1		
Help for others, work for others	6.3	8	6.6	8	6.3	8	5.9	7	6.1	8	6.6	8		
Leisure time spent together	4.3	3	4.2	4-5	4.9	5	5.2	5	4.1	3	4.9	5		
Personal character and moral qualities	5.0	5	6.0	7	5.0	6	6.4	8	5.2	5	5.6	7		

Note: The numbers in bold are the most significant discussed in the text

countries, they are also at the forefront, but with a lower percentage. The situation is different in Germany. The most common leisure time activity is reading (68%), followed by visits (42%), cinema (40%) and listening to music at home (33%). In Poland, most respondents watch TV in their free time (71%), followed by reading (63%). Other favourite activities are listening to music at home (47%) and visiting the cinema (44%). In Poland, most respondents prefer cultural but passive activities. In Slovakia, watching TV dominates (71%), but in the second place is gardening (58%), followed by reading (57%). Trips and walks are fourth (55%). In Ukraine, the most frequent activity is once again watching TV (64%), followed immediately by reading (62%). Visits (39%) and garden work (33%) are also popular.

Table 4.11 Leisure time activities of parents (in %)

Which leisure time activities are typical for you						
	The Czech Republic	Latvia	Germany	Poland	Slovakia	Ukraine
Reading	**60**	**72**	**68**	**63**	**57**	**62**
Music (actively)	13	14	23	12	17	19
Concerts (visit)	17	45	28	10	17	25
Theatre (visit)	24	41	32	15	17	29
Cinema (visit)	29	23	**40**	**44**	28	32
Handicraft	26	41	23	10	31	27
DIY	19	12	27	6	20	18
Gardening	**51**	**70**	23	31	**58**	**33**
Watching TV	**60**	**75**	32	**71**	**71**	**64**
Music (listening at home)	32	48	**33**	**47**	42	29
Disco, wine bars, restaurants	23	18	31	30	32	24
Visits	28	27	**42**	38	31	**39**
Trips, walks	**56**	**58**	18	41	**55**	26
Sport	38	40	32	19	33	14
Board games	9	17	12	8	14	3

Note: The numbers in bold are the most significant discussed in the text

An interesting comparison brings a comparison of the participation of respondents from individual countries in given leisure time activities. The most devoted to reading are Latvians and the least Slovaks. The most active in performing music are the Germans and Ukrainians. Concert and theatre visits are most represented in Latvia, while the least in Poland. Cinema is a favourite activity among Germans and Polish people. Handicraft enjoys the greatest popularity in Latvia, while DIY in Germany. Watching TV is almost the most popular leisure activity in all the countries except Germany. In Germany, only 32% of respondents chose this option, which is half less than in other countries. As far as visits and similar social activities are concerned, they are mostly realized in Germany, Ukraine and Poland. Trips and walks are popular in Latvia and in the Czech Republic, and on the contrary, they do not have much fans in Germany (only 18%).

In addition to choosing the leisure activities themselves, respondents were also asked to determine whether they pursue the activity themselves, with family members or friends. The results are shown in Table 4.12. For each activity, it is differentiated with whom respondents carry the activity. Column (a) means that the respondents carry out the activity themselves, (b) is with a family member, (c) is with friends. The most frequently chosen option for each activity and country is highlighted in

Table 4.12 Leisure time activities of parents (in %) divided into individual x family x with friends

Which leisure time activities are typical for you																		
	The Czech Republic			Latvia			Germany			Poland			Slovakia			Ukraine		
	(a)	(b)	(c)	(a)	(b)	(c)	(a)	(b)	(c)	(a)	(b)	(c)	(a)	(b)	(c)	(a)	(b)	(c)
Reading	53	6	0	62	10	0	58	9	1	54	9	0	53	4	0	57	4	1
Music (actively)	5	6	2	4	7	3	10	6	6	9	3	0	9	3	5	11	3	5
Concerts (visit)	2	9	6	4	32	9	0	12	17	1	5	4	1	4	12	3	11	12
Theatre (visit)	1	18	5	5	28	8	0	17	15	1	9	5	1	9	7	2	17	10
Cinema (visit)	1	22	6	1	19	2	0	18	22	3	32	9	1	10	17	3	17	13
Handicraft	22	3	1	37	4	0	21	1	1	9	1	0	24	6	0	24	2	1
DIY	14	5	4	9	3	0	6	19	1	4	2	0	10	10	0	12	5	1
Gardening	18	33	0	23	46	1	6	15	1	6	24	1	16	42	0	10	23	0
WatchingTV	8	52	0	16	59	0	1	30	1	14	56	1	8	62	1	12	51	1
Music (listening at home)	18	14	1	22	26	1	13	15	5	24	20	3	24	15	2	19	8	2
Disco, wine bars, restaurants	2	7	15	1	12	6	1	9	21	3	12	15	2	5	26	1	8	15
Visits	1	16	11	5	13	9	4	21	18	2	25	11	1	22	7	3	24	12
Trips, walks	3	49	4	6	46	6	1	14	3	5	30	6	6	37	12	2	17	7
Sport	12	21	5	18	19	3	12	6	14	6	9	4	14	12	6	8	4	2
Board games	0	7	2	2	13	3	1	6	4	1	4	3	1	8	5	1	1	1

Note: The numbers in bold are the most significant discussed in the text

colour (yellow = the possibility that respondents do the activity themselves; green = activity with family members; blue = activity with friends).

Table 4.12 shows that, across countries, some leisure time activities are purely individual, while others are most often implemented with family members or friends.

Individual activities include reading and handicrafts in all countries. This is not clear for other activities. Except Germany, the DIY is also individual, just in Germany it is an activity shared with family members. In four countries, active music playing is most individually performed, but in two it is most often with family members. It is similar with listening to music at home.

The activities that are clearly mostly together with other family members are: watching TV, gardening, visiting the theatre, visits, trips, walking and playing board games. It could be said that these activities strengthen family cohesion in all the countries under review, ensuring common experiences for family members. In almost all countries, this also applies to cultural events such as concerts and cinema visits. The most varied were activities that are most often carried out together with friends. Except of Latvia, there was some kind of leisure time activity in each country that respondents prefer to engage with friends. Most often, it is a visit to entertainment venues such as discos, wine bars, restaurants, etc. In Germany and Slovakia, respondents prefer to visit concerts and cinemas also with friends and Ukrainians also prefer to attend concerts with friends. The most interesting are the differences in the perception of the sport category. In two countries, sport is the most individual activity; in three countries, it is most practiced with family members; and in Germany, it is most often an activity practiced with friends.

The table shows in bold the three most frequently performed activities with family members (green fields) in each country. It is positive that at least one of the three most common family leisure time activities has an active character (trips, gardening, DIY, etc.)

References

Bendl, S., et al. (2015). *Vychovatelství: učebnice teoretickj5ch základů oboru*. Praha: Grada.

Český statistický úřad. (2018). Ne všechny státy stárnou stejne rychle.https://www.czso.cz/csu/czso/ne-vsechny-staty-starnou-stejne-rychle. Accessed 2 May 2019.

Dumazedier, J. (1962). *Vers une civilisation du loisir?* Paris: Editions du Seuil.

Dumazedier, J. (1966). Volnj5 čas. *Sociologick' časopis/Czech Sociological Review, 2*(3), 443–447.

Hofbauer, B. (2004). *Děti, mládež a volnj5 čas*. Praha: Portál.

Hofbauer, B. (2010). *Kapitoly z pedagogiky volného času*. České Budejovice: Jihočeská univerzita.

Hovorková, K. (2018). Pet t'dnů dovolené: nárok pro všechny, nebo jen benefit? V Evrope sepravidla různí. https://zpravy.aktualne.cz/finance/jak-jsme-na-tom-s-dovolenou-v-porovnani-s-ostatnimi-staty/r~69fa9456f96311e8bf040cc47ab5f122/. Accessed 26 June 2019.

Kaplánek, M. (Ed.). (2012). *Čas volnosti – čas vj5chovy*. Praha: Portál.

Kaplánek, M., et al. (2017). *Volnj5 čas a jeho vj5znam ve vj5chově*. Praha: Portál.

Knotová, D. (2011). *Pedagogické dimenze volného času*. Brno: Paido.

Kolesárová, K. (2016). *Životní styl v informační společnosti*. Praha: Univerzita Jana Amose Komenského Praha.

Kratochvílová, E. (2004). *Pedagogika voľného času: Vj5chova v čase mimo vyučovania v pedagogickej teórii a v praxi*. Bratislava: Univerzita Komenského v Bratislave.

Kraus, B., et al. (2015). *Životní styl současné české rodiny*. Hradec Králové: Gaudeamus.

Němec, J., et al. (2002). *Kapitoly ze sociální pedagogiky a pedagogiky volného času*. Brno: Paido.

Pávková, J., et al. (2002). *Pedagogika volného času: Teorie, praxe a perspektivy výchovy mimo vyučování a zařízení volného času*. Praha: Portál.

Sak, P. (2000). *Proměny české mládeže*. Praha: Petrklíč.

Sak, P., & Saková, K. (2004). *Mládež na křižovatce*. Praha: Svoboda Servis.

Stašová, L., Slaninová, G., & Junová, I. (2015). *Nová generace*. Hradec Králové: Gaudeamus.

The Convention on the Rights of the Child. (1989). https://www.unicef.org/child-rights-convention/convention-text. Accessed 23 June 2019.

The Universal Declaration of Human Rights. https://www.un.org/en/universal-declaration-human-rights/. Accessed 23 June 2019.

The World Leisure Organization. (2001). *The charter for leisure in the year*. https://worldleisure.org/wp-content/uploads/2018/04/International_Charter_For_LeisureWEB-1.pdf. Accessed 23 June 2019.

Vážanský, M. (2001). *Základy pedagogiky volného času*. Brno: Print – Typia.

Veselá, J. (1999). *Základy sociologie volného času*. Pardubice: Univerzita Pardubice.

Chapter 5
Media in the Lives of Contemporary Families

Abstract The chapter on media in family life highlights the aspects of lifestyle of contemporary families in the context of the saturation of households with modern means of communication, their usage and attitudes towards them. Considerable attention was paid to the issue of family-related media in current research, as evidenced by a wide range of studies and research surveys. This chapter is devoted to several partial aspects of this attention and is based on the data of two surveys. The first research is the European representative survey Eurobarometer 88 (Eurobarometer 2017), and the other one is our research on the Lifestyle of the Contemporary Family (further LSCF, 2012–2015). These data shows an extension of selected media facilities in families, their usage and media leisure time activities and attitudes towards media. The studied countries are in some respects very similar to each other (relatively strong media saturation of households, most common daily use of television and computers, positive perception of media as a way to facilitate communication and negotiation). In other respects (joint media activities, strength of perception of negative aspects of media, usage of media by parents and by children), the countries differ.

Keywords Family · Media · Lifestyle · Leisure time · Media research · Electronic media · European families · Parents · Children · Family system · Socialization · Family upbringing

5.1 Media Research in the Context of Family Issues

In recent years, the issue of the media and the contemporary family has received increasing attention in many scientific disciplines. It is initiated both by massive expansion of media types and their rapid penetration into the space of the contemporary family and its lifestyle, but also by discussions of the influence that the media have in the environment of the contemporary family. Current families in developed countries have been gradually described as "**media-rich homes**" for more than a decade (Livingstone 2002). The speed of media saturation in contemporary families varies across countries and social strata. However, what is certain is that despite the diversity of such saturation of the family environment, this changes the life of

© The Author(s) 2020   87
B. Kraus et al., *Contemporary Family Lifestyles in Central and Western Europe*,
SpringerBriefs in Sociology, https://doi.org/10.1007/978-3-030-48299-2_5

the contemporary family, its lifestyle, communication, culture and the whole family system. The changing family environment in connection with media coverage began to be emphasized, especially in recent decades, when a number of new modern media began to emerge also in families and households (e.g. Livingstone 2002; Watkins 2009; Jenkins et al. 2009; Turkle 2011; Vittrup et al. 2016). Massive media coverage of the society, coupled with a fall in the price of individual media devices, has allowed them to penetrate into households and families in increasing quantities.

Another major change that accompanies the media coverage of today's households is the change in media localization (Livingstone 2002; Hagen 2007). With the increasing number of household appliances, the so-called bedroom culture has begun to emerge, reflecting the shift of TV and computers into the private rooms of individual household members, i.e. nurseries, bedrooms, study rooms, etc. While according to Livingstone (2002), the fundamental problem of families was where to place individual media and whether to equip children's rooms with television or not, the emergence of new mobile media takes the meaning out of these questions. That is because these new mobile media allow individual family members (therefore children as well) to carry them anywhere at any time (e.g. Roberts and Foehr 2008).

The multiplicity and mobility of media at home also brings an ever-greater privatization in the sphere of media use (especially for children), individualization of leisure time activities and declining social control that parents can realize towards children. The worlds within the family can thus distance from each other.

Hagen (2007, p. 372) states that *"Children's rooms are an arena in which children can use the media at their own deliberation to pursue their own lifestyle. Households are gradually becoming a space in which people live together, but separately/individually. Parental control becomes the more complicated, the more media resources children have in their private rooms."* Yet in 2012, Coyne et al. note that attention to the way how families use media and how they are influenced by it is still inadequate. Although since then a large number of studies on various aspects of the family and the media have been carried out, the question is whether the mapping of this area can already be perceived as sufficient. That is because research on this subject is quite quickly outdated and its results are usually quickly surpassed. The development of new media and its reflection in social reality usually have a faster gradient than the possibilities of social research and the publication of its results. Another trend, that we can observe is the gradual multiplication of the functions of individual media. The new media are no longer dedicated to the chosen purpose, but allow more functions—communication, entertainment, office replacement, navigation in an environment, etc.

In relation to **the lifestyle of a family** and its individual members, Livingstone (2002) points to a decline in so-called street culture and to the growth of media-rich households and the privatization of media consumption. He states that children's leisure time activities have gradually shifted from freely accessible places outside the family to the households themselves. This has changed the nature of childhood and the life of the whole family. The usual reasons for such a shift mentioned by parents reflect the sense of danger that the child faces in the streets and outdoors. On the contrary, the home is then understood as a safe place (e.g. Livingstone 2002;

Gondová 2014). Arguments of children to justify more time spent at home (and hence in the media) tend to involve pointing out at claimed smaller range of options for active and interesting ways of spending leisure time away from home. However, even when children spend time with their peers away from home, they often tend to spend time together with the media at their friends' homes. The media thus largely concentrated the lives of individuals from the public to the private—to the household and family. However, at the same time, an individualization of leisure time at home happened and as well as a shift from the family's private space to the "public space" of the virtual media world. Physically, family members are present in a common space, but their minds are in worlds, which are distant and different from each other. Turkle talks about **new intimacy and new loneliness** (2011).

Analysing the social potential of the media is another important part of their research. It can be assumed that the media in the family space not only play the role of means of leisure time fun, easier communication, home office and other activities, but that their reach goes even further. Reeves and Nass (1998) applied knowledge of personality psychology in their researches in the 1990s and concluded that people treat the media as real people, things and places. People treat the media thoughtfully, media can have their "personality", evoke emotional relationships, demand attention, influence memories and change ideas about what is natural. The media thus become full participants in our social and biological world. Media personality is perceived as a *real personality*, the media evoke the *same emotions* as in a real situation, and the media experience of an individual is *an emotional experience.* (e.g., Geraghty 1996; Reeves and Nass 1998). In this sense, we could think of media as of other "household members" and that many virtual media characters or media situations are real in their social reach. Turkle (2011) points out at how the use of new media that work with the "be online" status changes social relationships. That is because generations of children growing up in this virtual relationship environment expect less from relationships.

Theoretical views of the media and family is usually based **on several intertwining theories** that are internally consistent. Most authors rely on systemic approaches to family study, supplemented by knowledge of family development theories or environmental perspectives (e.g. Dalope and Woods 2018). In some publications, media analysis is carried out in the context of the so-called multitheoretical model (e.g. Hertlein 2012). It is primarily an analysis of the importance of technology in partner and family life. This model is based on the interconnection of three theories—perspective of family ecology, structural-functionalist perspective and interaction-constructist perspective.

The environmental approach focuses on the ways how the environment affects family life and the fact that environmental impacts can be reflected in two types of relationship changes—both in the structure of relationships and in family processes. A number of media researchers (e.g. Livingstone 2002) point out at a change in the ecological perspective of today's family, which was highly affected by electronic media. While a few decades ago many electronic media were absent from families or were present only to a limited extent (television, radio), the massive emergence of new media into the private spaces of today's homes has completely changed the environment in which today's families live, realize relationships among its members and socialize new generations. Buermann emphasizes the fact that, in contemporary families' television, like other media, "has expanded the space of the family in a way and created new spaces" (2009, p. 41).

Numerous studies are focused at the way how are media usually used by individuals (*normative media use*) within and outside of the family, with frequent accent mainly on children and teenagers (e.g. Zabriskie and McCormick 2001; Gentile and Walsh 2002; Roberts and Foehr 2008, etc.). However, a number of researches have analysed the use of media and the frequency of it without taking into account context of a family and without linking it to other circumstances of lives of the surveyed people. Most of these studies point to out at the increasing amount of time, which children and young people spend these days in front of television screens, computers, social networks, etc. (e.g. Sak and Kolesárová 2004; Roberts and Foehr 2008). The Dutch study by Nikken (2017) points out at the fact that higher or lower level of use of media in the family is related to these basic characteristics of the family—"education level, number of screens at home, time spent by children on media, type of media content used, ease of mediation, views on media for children" (2017, 1).

Other studies provide an insight into the way how the media influence family habits and leisure time activities of families (e.g., Vanderwater et al. 2005; Jordan et al. 2006). The media explosion in families has caused them to change the way they use media, and it also changed the impact media has on individuals and the entire family system (Padilla-Walker et al. 2012). While some believe that the effect of the media is a process of individualization and individuals in the family are becoming more distant (e.g. Turkle 2011), others argue that the media has become an integral part of the lifestyle of the family and that they can have both positive and negative effects on the functioning of a family (e.g. Hoover et al. 2004; Takeuchi 2011, etc.). Some researches show how family cohesion, communication between members of a family and mutual cooperation are increased through diverse media (e.g. Padilla-Walker et al. 2012; Coyne et al. 2014; Torrecillas-Lacave et al. 2017).

Authors also quite often rely on theories of family development (e.g. Davies and Gentile 2012; Coyne et al. 2014) and assume that families at different stages of development, with respect to the number and age of children, use the media differently, develop different habits and strategies for their use. This also affects family processes and relationships. According to the research, more positive media habits are associated with families in the early stages of development, in families with more children and in families where there are greater differences in the age of siblings (Davies and Gentile 2012). Television socialization of preschool children has been addressed, for example, by Šeďová (2007), who points out at the fact that preschool children usually have to fully comply with their parents with the use of television and their wishes enter family habits as an intervening variable. Other surveys on media education in families clearly show that age is an important variable that determines the degree of parental intervention and the perception of its need. The older children are, the less parents restrict them from using electronic media and they also feel that it is not that much needed. Greater regulation and media monitoring can be found in families with younger children (Stašová et al. 2012). Many researchers pay particular attention to families with children of adolescence (Padilla-Walker et al. 2012, etc.) System theories make it possible to perceive media as part of the family system and to assume that interactions between individuals in the family create an open and evolving system that is continually influenced by the environment, which in this case contains the media and its influences. The media is perceived as one of many environmental influences, which is reflected in family interactions and may even play a role in redefining family processes or be integrated as part of family patterns or created rules (Livingstone 2002). Everyday family interactions over time create habits, rituals and meanings and contribute to creating a common history and reality sharing. An interesting recent contribution to the study of media in the family is also the study of the use of television during meals with families with preschool children. Wenhold and Harrison (2018) tried to analyse families with a higher and low proportion of watching TV at mealtime and ritualization at mealtime, as well as harmony at mealtime and children's food composition.

The use of media within a family can create "collective memory" (Broderick 1993) and also allow "co-orientation", which occurs when more people concentrate on the same object in their environment and evaluate it (Koerner and Fitzpatrick 2006). Even though, there may be different social perceptions of each of the actors, the very fact of co-orientation can increase family cohesion in the activity itself. Sharing the media is thus reflected in family cohesion and contributes to maintaining family relationships. The usage in the family is usually dependent on the child's age and the socio-demographic characteristics of the parents, such as education, gender and family structure.

The lifestyle of the family also includes the aspect of the possible gaming media activities. As a significant predictor of playing video games was shown an active-recreational orientation of family (Tobias 2017). For example, Gee et al. (2017) were focused on playing video games in the family, and they pointed out at the fact that media-related gaming and learning can be understood in three contexts—playing video games with accent on *digital medium*, playing video games like *a game* and playing video games as a *family practice, family ritual*. In each of these perspectives, *learning* also has different positions and meanings. New work by Taylor et al. (2018) has also studied the analysis of ways in which family can learn together through mobile technology.

The interest in modern media, especially electronic social networks, raises sensitive attention. Ünal (2018) focuses on effects, which social networking has on the time spent with family members. For example, it was shown in his work, that "three fourth of the participants logged into Facebook in the presence of other family member. Moreover, most of the participants reported that their partner ignores them and their children due to excessive time spent on Facebook." (Ünal 2018, 362) Another modern electronic medium was studied by Yu et al. (2018), which pointed out at the role of smartphones in the field of family leisure time and, above all, at the level of common holidays. Leisure time is precisely what the family can use to improve family interaction and cohesion. Qualitative research by the authors has shown that families rely on smartphones as tools that enable them to do both, to maintain family unity while preserving the individuality of its members. Smartphones also conveyed family experiences from a place of staying and altered traditional internalization and the process of preserving holiday memories.

In recent researches, considerable attention has been paid to the relationship between parents and children in the area of common media use. Padilla-Walker et al. (2012) point out at the different ways of how a family with adolescent children uses the media and how it strengthens the family cohesion (also Torrecillas-Lacave et al. 2017). For example, the use of mobile phones among family members is associated with greater family cohesion, parents' awareness and peace of parents (also Green 2008; Weisskirch 2009). An inspirational topic, that could also be given more attention, is the use of media in an extended family, maintaining relationships with grandparents or other relatives. Interesting contributions to the study of media in the context of the present family are also analysis of how media are used in transition situations, especially when entering parenthood (Nathansons and Manohar 2012; Bartholomew et al. 2012). Unfortunately, other transitional situations in the family on the side of parents or children remain aside from greater attention.

5.2 Electronic Media in European Families

The field of use of electronic media and attitudes towards them was included in some of the abovementioned surveys, it was also a part of our research into the lifestyle of the current family, and it was also mapped in the Eurobarometer 88 survey in 2017. This chapter is concerned on the situation in Europe in general and focused especially on countries included in our research. First of all, we use the data from Eurobarometer, and then we continue in analysis of the data from our research (LSCF). The goal is to compare situations and patterns in countries we are interested in and try to use the data from both analyses to describe some features of a picture of media in the lifestyle of contemporary family.

The only exception must be taken in the case of Ukraine, which has not been a respondent state of Eurobarometer survey. Therefore, we can use only data from our survey for Ukraine. Otherwise, into the Standard Eurobarometer 88 survey, which was conducted in 2017, there have been included 34 territories.[1]

Eurobarometer has shown that the most commonly used medium remains television. However, the most rapidly growing media used by the European citizens are the Internet and online social networks. Eighty-four percentage of Europeans watch it every day or almost every day. In comparison with the year 2016, it has been a growth of two percentage points. Television is mostly watched on the television set or on the Internet. Furthermore, the proportion of people watching it on the Internet has been rising continuously. Over more, 77% of Europeans use the Internet at least

---

[1] 28 Member States of the European Union, the five candidate countries and the Turkish Cypriot Community in the part of the country not controlled by the government of the Republic of Cyprus.

Table 5.1 Watching TV in families

	Watching TV on a television set		Watching TV via Internet	
	Every day or almost every day	Never	Every day or almost every day	Never
Czech Republic (%)	80	2	7	60
Germany (%)	78	2	15	59
Latvia (%)	71	8	16	48
Poland (%)	76	4	13	59
Slovakia (%)	81	2	8	63
The Ukraine (%)	Not included in Eurobarometer		Not included in Eurobarometer	

Source Eurobarometer (2017)

once a weak. Fifty-eight percentage of Europeans use the online social networks at least once a weak, and 42% of population use it every day or almost every day.

If we compare data from countries included in our research and their results in Eurobarometer, there can be found slight differences in watching TV on a *TV set* or *via Internet*. More than 80% of respondents watch television **on a TV set every day or almost every day** in Slovakia and Czech Republic, a lower proportion of 78% in Germany, 76% in Poland and 71% in Latvia.

Watching television **via Internet** every day or almost every day has been declared at these levels: Latvia 16%, Germany 15%, Poland 13%, Slovakia 8%, Czech Republic 7%. Therefore, Czech Republic and Slovakia could be labelled as more traditional in watching TV. Czech and Slovak people use more often television set in comparison with an access via Internet. In Germany and Latvia, the proportion of watching TV via Internet is double than in Czech Republic and Slovakia (Table 5.1).

Daily or almost daily use of a **radio** has varied widely from one state to another. It has been least common in Romania (24%) and the most common in Germany (72%). The other states included in our research have had following proportions of people who use the radio daily or almost daily: Latvia 50%, Slovakia 50%, Czech Republic 45%, Poland 44%.

Internet use continues to vary significantly from one-member state to another. According to Eurobarometer data, Slovakia belongs to countries with the lowest proportion of everyday use of the Internet—(52%). Czech Republic and Poland belong to another group of countries where the proportion is higher (55–63%). Otherwise, Germany and Latvia have been found in a group with the share between 64 and 71%. The European mean is 65%, and the higher use of the Internet has been declared by men (69%) than women (62%). According to this, we can see that only Germany and Latvia have occurred in the European mean level or a little bit higher—Germany 67% Latvia 71%.

As the Eurobarometer has shown, over four in ten Europeans (42%) say they use an **online social network** every day or almost every day. This proportion raised continuously over the last few years. Despite this, 35% of Europeans have declared that they had not been involved in online social networks, 32% have never used them and 3% said that they could not access them. Regarding the use of online social networks, there have been found significant differences among member states. In the Czech Republic and Germany, the daily use has achieved 32%; by contrast of it in Sweden, it has been 60% of respondents. The use of online social networks is on the rise in a large majority of studied countries, particularly in Poland and Bulgaria. On the other hand, it has fallen slightly in Ireland and in the Czech Republic. A significantly higher proportion of population in Latvia has declared that they use online social network every day or almost every day (53%) in the contrast with other countries included in our research.

More information about media at homes come from our research (LSCF). Our data showed that families in countries where our research was conducted differed in terms of media facilities. More than half of respondents in the Czech Republic, Poland, Slovakia and Ukraine reported higher levels of TV sets (i.e. two or more TV sets at home). On the other hand, households with no TV set were most prevalent in Germany, where almost a quarter of respondents said that they do not have a TV set (Fig. 5.1). This may be partly explained by data from the Eurobarometer 88, which showed that in Germany, for example, people use more Internet connections to watch television than a conventional television device. Our research data showed that all the German families we studied were equipped with a computer. Overall, computer equipment in households was high in the countries we reviewed. Only in Latvia, 11% of respondents said that they do not have a computer, and in Ukraine it was less than 3%. In other countries, the share of families without a computer was

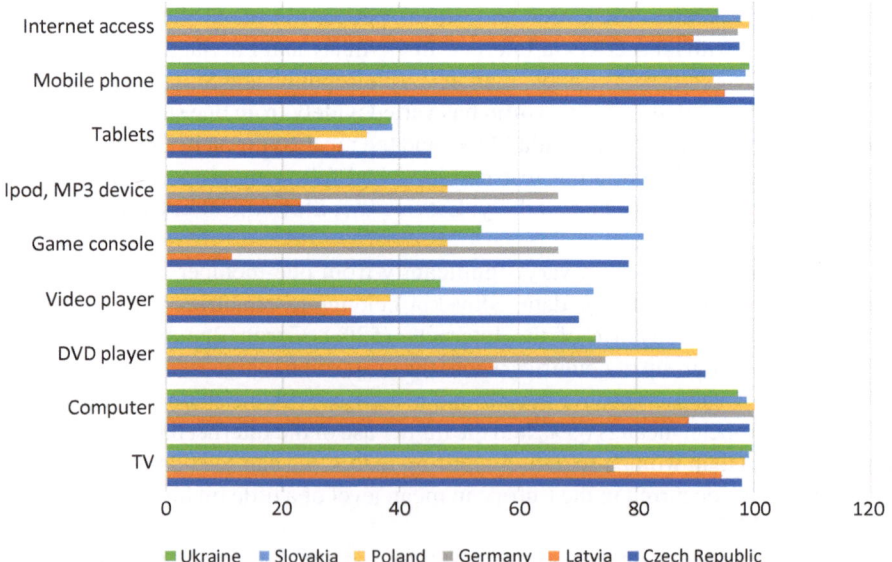

Fig. 5.1 Percentage of families equipped by media devices

Table 5.2 Internet access in families of the studied countries (percentage of households which reported the Internet access)

	Czech Republic	Latvia	Germany	Poland	Slovakia	The Ukraine
Yes	**97.6**	**89.7**	**97.3**	**99.2**	**97.8**	**93.8**
No	2.4	10.3	2.7	0.8	2.2	6.2
Total	100	100	100	100	100	100

negligible (up to 1%). Even more than half of households in all countries except Latvia had two or more computers. This was mostly the case of Slovakia, where the share of households with two or more computers was almost 71%. From this point of view, households' equipment of computers was higher than equipment of televisions. However, this may be related to the fact that in many cases television broadcasts can be viewed online on a computer, and the computers can thus well substitute the functions of the television.

The households we studied also showed considerable access to the Internet (Table 5.2), as the Eurobarometer data did. Paradoxically, in our research, the Internet access was the lowest in Latvia (less than 90% of households with the Internet access), while in the Eurobarometer survey the Latvian households used the Internet and social networks to a greater extent. However, it is possible, that due to the time gap between the collection of our survey data and the Eurobarometer survey, fundamental changes in the digitization of Latvian households occurred. On the other hand, differences may also be due to the fact that **access** to the Internet does not necessarily mean that households are actively **using** it.

In all other countries, the Internet access was above 90% and in Poland it was even 99%. High Internet access was probably also related to the fact that we interviewed households with children. Data from a number of surveys show that the presence of children at a household increases the presence of media and also the access to the Internet (e.g. Latvia. Statistics in Brief 2019; Czech Statistical Office 2019). Families often acquire these facilities because of children and to allow them to use media and the Internet for school preparation. Modern means of communication also represent for children a path of inclusion into peer groups.

In the studied families, it was a matter of course to own a mobile phone. Most households had more of these devices, which could also copy the number of household members who could use it. Paradoxically, in Germany only two-thirds of households reported two or more mobile phones in the household, while in other countries the proportion of such families was over 80%. However, this may also be related to the composition of households and the age of children in them.

Among the less represented media in the families belong DVD players. In Latvia, Germany and Ukraine, one quarter or more households did not have such a facility. On the contrary, two or more of these facilities had a part of Polish and German households (more than 15%) and about 13% of Czech families. Even less than DVD players occurred in families' video players. A large proportion of Latvian, German and Polish households did not have it at all (more than 60%). The presence of two or more video players was otherwise very low, ranging up to 5% of households in all countries studied.

Also, at the time of our investigation, the game consoles were probably still entering family homes. Their higher incidence was recorded in the Czech Republic and Germany, where at least one facility had around 40% of households. In the contrary, very few gaming consoles appeared in Latvia and Ukraine (88% of households did not have such a device at all).

IPod and MP3 players were most frequently found in the Czech Republic and Slovakia, where more than a third of households reported that they have at least two of them. On the other hand, the lowest number of facilities was in Latvia, Poland and Ukraine (52% and 46%).

At the time of the survey, the tablets also appeared to be entering European households. In fact, in all countries studied, more than half of the households had no such a device at all.

5.3   Media Activities as Part of Spending Leisure Time

Another part of our questionnaire was directed to the use of media and activities of families around them. Therefore, we asked respondents who from the family uses the media equipment the most. Some media devices were shown to be highly **parental** across the spectrum of countries studied (such as television), and some were used more **by children** (tablets, games consoles, IPods and MP3 devices) (Figs. 5.2 and 5.3).

While in Germany computers and tablets were predominantly parental media, in many other countries (except the Czech Republic) they were used more by children. In Polish households, DVD and video players were clearly the parental media, while in other countries they were used by both—parent and children and were both used on a similar level. Game consoles, IPods, MP3 players and tablets were clearly used more by children in Czech households. Also in Ukrainian households, the main users of IPods, MP3 players and tablets were children. A certain exception was observed in Slovak households.

Some facilities did not show a clear tendency, as the proportion of children and parents using them was close to 50%. It was both parental and children's media—as, for example, computers.

In terms of the frequency of media use in households, it was possible to follow trends from our research that were also confirmed by the Eurobarometer survey. **Every day**, the interviewed families used most often **television and computers**. The use of television even (with the exception of Germany) outweighed the use of computers. In Germany, there was a slightly different pattern of using media devices,

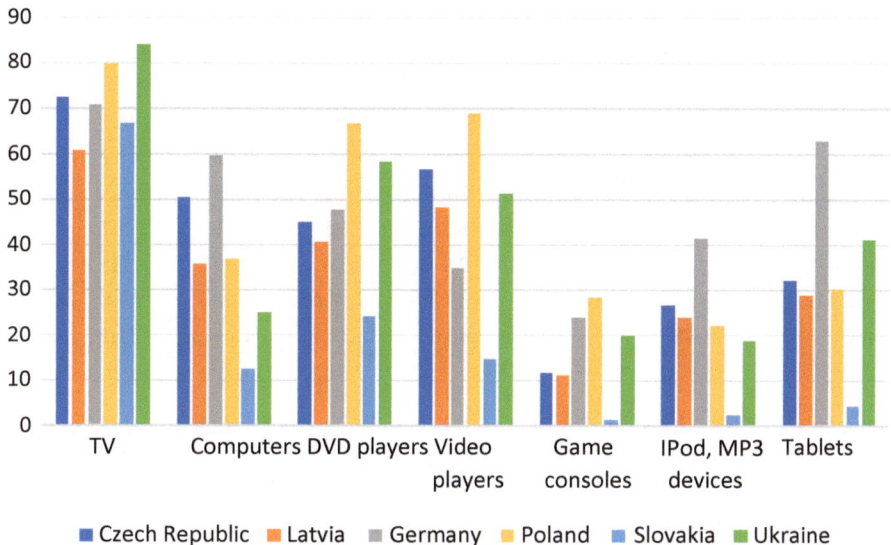

Fig. 5.2 Percentage of families where selected media devices are used mainly by parents

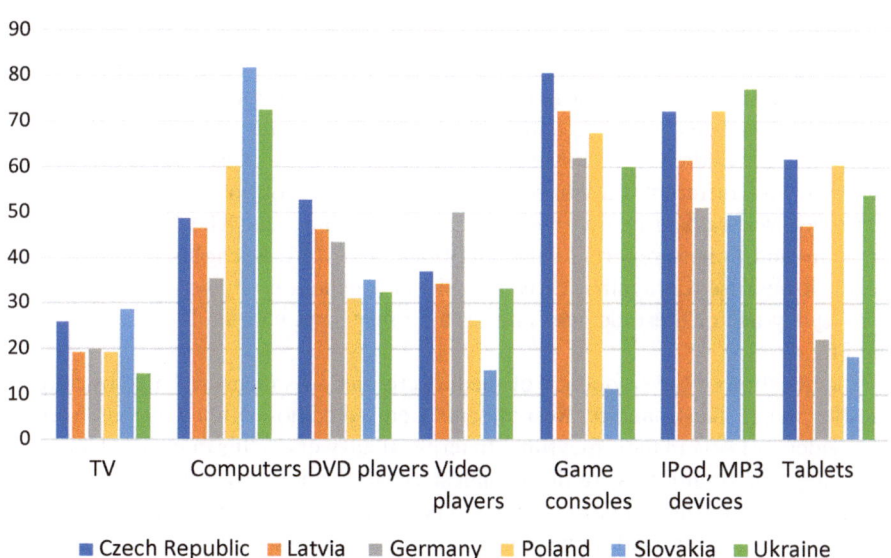

Fig. 5.3 Percentage of families where selected media devices are used mainly by children

Table 5.3 Daily use of selected media devices

	The Czech Republic	Latvia	Germany	Poland	Slovakia	The Ukraine
TV	89.4	85.3	75.4	76	92.3	92.7
PC	83.8	81	89	75.2	92.2	87.7
DVD player	5.9	11.9	16.4	5	2.8	6.5
Video player	2.3	2.6	3.7	1.5	2.1	5.2
Gaming console	10	8.5	2.9	3.8	1.7	5.5
IPod, MP3 player	20	32.7	30.2	18.6	11.2	54.8
Tablet	48.3	63.6	40.6	32.7	13.4	71.1

because there was lower level of TV sets equipment but much higher computer equipment. It can be assumed that this is also the reason why the daily activities related to the use of computers were higher in Germany (Table 5.3).

Less frequently used media were, due to the lower level of their equipment, video players and game consoles (only 1.5% of households to 10% of households used them every day). Most of these facilities were used in the Czech Republic, Latvia and Ukraine.

The daily use of IPods, MP3 players and tablets showed some differences. Quite surprisingly, the highest shares of daily use of these devices occurred in Ukrainian households. About a third of the households, which were equipped with these devices, used them every day in Latvia and Germany. On the contrary, the Czech Republic, Poland and Slovakia had the lowest proportions of their daily use. The use of tablets was somewhat different. Latvia, where nearly two-thirds of households used tablets every day, was ranked behind the abundant Ukrainian uses. The Czech Republic, Germany and Poland reported between 30 and 40% of households with daily use, and the lowest use was again in Slovakia. Slovakia generally showed the lowest share of everyday use of these devices and on the other hand had the highest use of TV and PC.

The question of the frequency of media activities was measured also by another question in our questionnaire. Respondents were asked how often they watch television, video or DVD in their free time. In terms of answers to this question, Ukrainian and Latvian households were the strongest viewers, with over 40% of respondents saying they were watching more than two hours a day. On the contrary, respondents from Germany and Poland showed the least time spent by watching these facilities. It was also interesting that in Germany there was the strongest group of those who did not watch these facilities at all (11%). Again, this may be related to the fact that in Germany, the Internet was also used more for watching TV than in other countries.

A question about the frequency of gaming (whether on a computer or via the Internet) showed that the strongest players were again respondents from Ukraine and Slovakia. These countries had the highest proportions of respondents who reported playing more than 2 hours a day. In the Ukraine, it was almost 50%, in Slovakia 38% (Fig. 5.4).

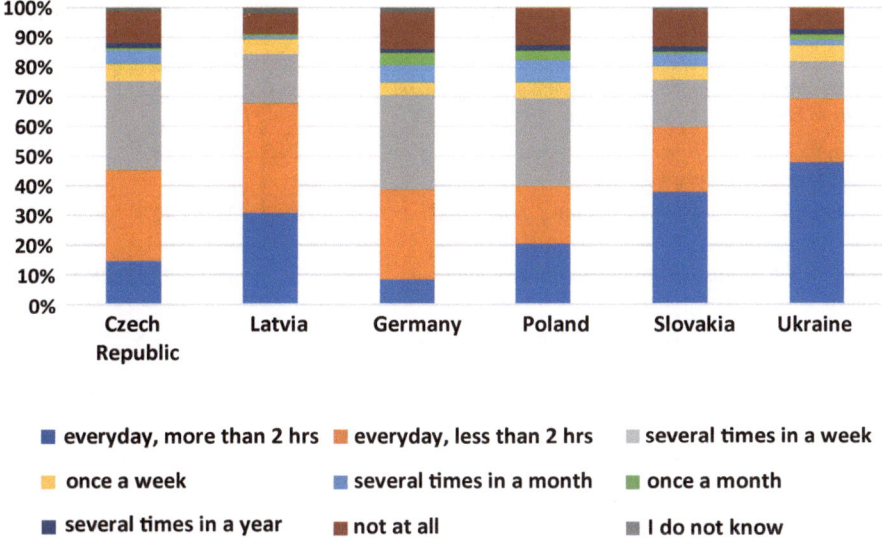

Fig. 5.4 How often you play on a computer or via the Internet?

Gaming was the least declared in Germany (8%) and in the Czech Republic (14%). Very interesting was also the proportion of those who declared that they do not play at all. It was comparable for a number of countries (Czech Republic, Germany, Poland, Slovakia 10–13%) and Latvia and Ukraine (6–7%). The group of "weaker players" included the Czech Republic, Germany and Poland as countries with a lower proportion of leisure time playing, while Slovakia and Ukraine showed a higher frequency of gaming activities.

It would be also interesting to create further analyses of what kind of households are the interviewed families, what is their lifestyle and what are other circumstances that lead to the media activities of these family that they do not play computer games at all. Some studies show that playing computer games is usually more of an activity of children or a joint activity of fathers and their sons.

In the next question, our research was focused on respondents' attitudes and agreement or disagreement with some statements concerning electronic media in households. Respondents were presented with a set of statements on which they expressed positions on a four-point scale, from "very agree" to "very disagree". They were not offered the middle variant and always had to choose positive or negative view towards the statement.

We could again observe some similarities and differences of studied households. Overall, our respondents were most in favour of these statements: "*The electronic media we have at home makes it easier for us to communicate and to agree with each other*" and "*The electronic media we have at home allows us to be independent*". Equally positive was the view of the statement "*The media we have at home allows us to be able to focus on our own hobbies and our own entertainment*" (Table 5.4). Our

Table 5.4 Attitudes of respondents towards the media (percentage of consent to the statement)

	CZ	LV	DE	PL	SK	UA
The electronic media we have at home makes it easier for us to communicate and to agree with each other	77.8	64.6	51.4	85.5	81.6	57.7
We argue with each other at home often because of the media (television, computer, etc.)	13.8	**24.3**	17.2	18.5	**21.3**	**23.7**
Media are a good mean which allows us to spend our free time together	29.2	36.1	24.2	46.4	36.7	67
Home media distance us from each other within our family	38.4	31.8	**46.4**	32.5	**48.4**	30.3
The electronic media we have at home allows us to be independent	57.2	60.6	57.4	57.8	54.9	46
We spend more time with media (television, computer, etc.) than with talking with each other at home	39.3	**48.7**	34.4	39.8	**52.8**	**47.2**
If we had no media at home (television, computer, etc.) our life would be better	27.0	21.8	21.6	21.8	**32.5**	19.8
The media we have at home allow us to be able to focus on our own hobbies and our own entertainment	45.9	**65.7**	35.7	**63.2**	53.3	**71.9**

Note: The numbers in bold are the most significant discussed later in the text

respondents significantly pointed out at the advantages and positives of the media and what they allowed them to do. It was just mentioned the facilitation of communication, independence and the opportunity to engage in hobbies and entertainment. Respondents from Ukraine, Slovakia and Poland strongly reflected the media as a factor enabling them to pursue their hobbies and their entertainment.

The media as a source of *a distance between family members* was also reflected in Germany and in Slovakia almost in half of households. Agreement with the statement that *"we spend more time with media than with talking with each other at home"* was the strongest in Latvia, Slovakia and Ukraine, where about half of the families surveyed agreed with the statement. The strongest agreement with the statement *"If we had no media at home our life would be better."* was registered with Slovak families (almost one third of respondents), the second country where its respondents expressed stronger agreement with this statement was the Czech Republic (27%). Disputes in the family as a result of the influence of media in the family were most often declared by respondents from Latvia, Slovakia and Ukraine. These were also the countries in which respondents also agreed most with the statement that they spend more time with the media than with communication within the family. The countries in which we can perceive a stronger perception of the negative impact of the media were Latvia, Slovakia and Ukraine. With regard to theoretical approaches, our data confirm both the hypothesis of the negative impact of the media on the family life and also its positive benefits (e.g. Padilla-Wlker et al. 2012; Torrecillas-lava et al. 2017; Yu et al. 2018).

Table 5.5 Do you ever play computer games together?

	The Czech Republic	Latvia	Germany	Poland	Slovakia	The Ukraine
Yes, very often	**2.6**	**2.7**	**2.7**	**2.4**	**2.4**	**3.7**
Yes, often	29.2	29.1	22.7	40.3	25.1	28.4
No, never	**68.2**	**68.2**	**74.7**	**57.3**	**72.5**	**67.8**
Total	100	100	100.1	100	100	99.9

Note: The numbers in bold are the most significant discussed later in the text

5.4 Joint Media Activities in Leisure Time of Families

Another interesting area that we had the opportunity to watch in our data was some common media activities in the family, namely the **joint playing of computer games and the joint watching of television**, especially during leisure time. These are the media that are most commonly used in families, and we asked if family-related media activities are also done together with other members of the family. In all countries, the share of families who very often play together on a computer or on the Internet ranged only from 2 to 4%. It was the highest in Ukraine (3.7%). The highest proportion of families ever playing computer games together (either very often or occasionally) was among Polish families (42.4%). On the other hand, Germany and Slovakia were the populations where computer gaming was declared the least, with more than 70% of the families which surveyed that they never play together. Overall, playing games was not a very common activity of the studied sample of European families (Table 5.5).

Another question in the questionnaire (30 hb), which included computer and Internet gaming during free time, confirmed that gaming is mostly an activity that respondents do independently. Playing together with another family member was the most common in Ukrainian (40%) and Polish households (20%).

This was different with watching TV, almost 50% of households in Slovakia, Poland and Latvia reported that they watch TV together very often (Fig. 5.5). Households in the Czech Republic and Ukraine mentioned TV activity as slightly less common, and watching TV together was the least common in Germany, where the share of families who never watch TV together was 17.6%. This might be related to the fact that in Germany not that many households are equipped with TV sets in general and there was also a lower use of television recorded.

Yet in another question (30 gb) of our questionnaire, it was possible to see if respondents reported watching TV, video or DVD together. The fact that they watch these media together with a family member in their free time **was most often mentioned by Czech and Slovak respondents**, and the least by Latvian households.[2]

---

[2]Results for Latvian households are partly in contradictory to the findings of the previous question, where respondents from Latvia reported very common watching TV together. However, this could be due to the inclusion of additional media in question 30 g that could have influenced the respondents' answers.

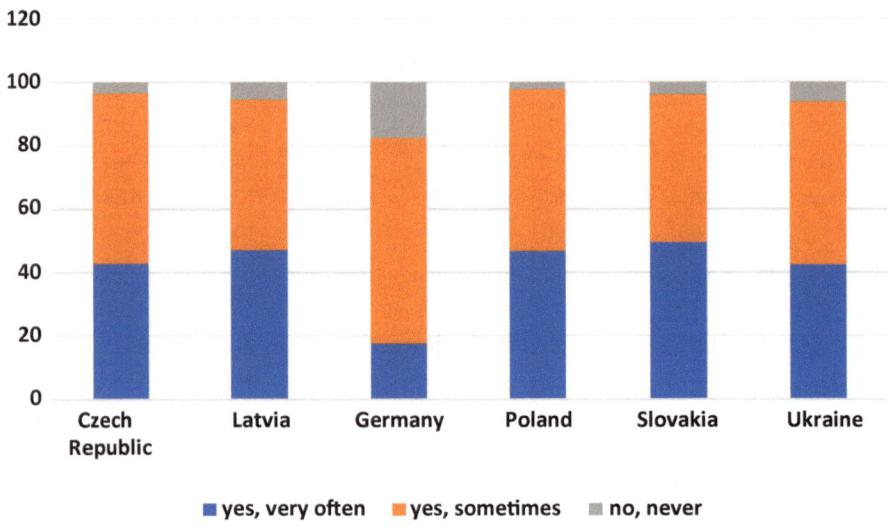

Fig. 5.5 Do you ever watch TV at home together?

In households where family watches TV together, we were also interested in **what types of family programmes are most often watched together**.[3] Czech and Polish households were most interested in watching documentary and educational programmes. Czech, Ukrainian and Slovak families were most interested in news and journalism. Overall, families across the countries studied mostly watched films and series together. Czech households were more interested in sports and music programmes and together with Slovak households, in entertainment programmes.

If we look at watching TV programs together with a family through the country's optics, we can see that in **Slovakia** the joint watching television included mostly news and journalism, films and series and entertainment. In **Ukraine**, it was mainly news and journalism, with a slightly lower frequency of films and series, and there was also an abundance of statements that families were watching everything, the type of programme did not matter. **Polish** families watched mostly documentary and educational programmes and films and series. In **Germany**, between the mostly watched TV programmes together were included documentary and educational programmes, films and then news and journalism, with a similar intensity of series. In Czech families, there were highly watched most of the types of programmes.

According to a number of surveys, family activities create and increase family cohesion. Joint media activities may also contribute to this (e.g. Koerner and Fitzpatrick 2006; Broderick 1993; Coyne et al. 2014). Therefore, contemporary families can realize the necessary component of sharing and spending their free time together through appropriately chosen media activities. At the same time, parents can also

---

[3]Unfortunately, we do not have data from Latvian households for this question.

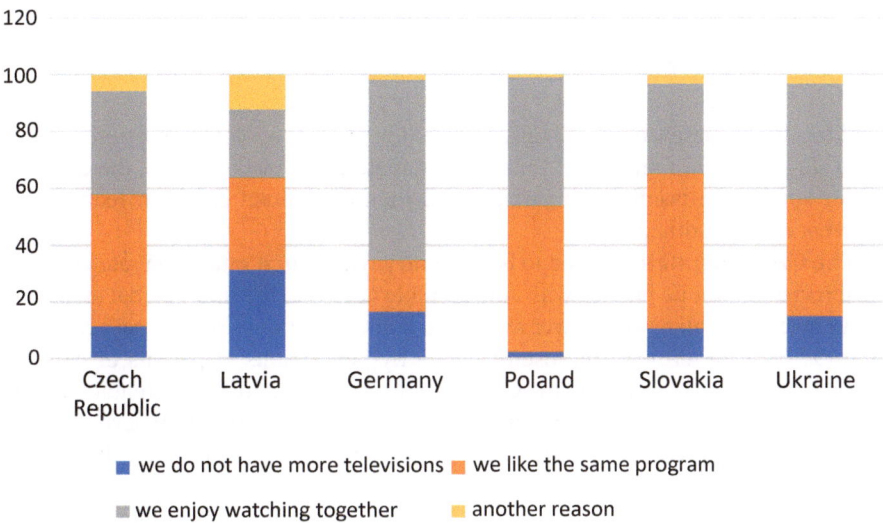

Fig. 5.6 Main reasons of watching TV together

non-violently implement some elements of media education and approach the world of their children plus find common communication topics.

In our research, we also tried to uncover the reasons for watching TV together (Fig. 5.6). In the Czech Republic, Poland and Slovakia, it was because respondents **liked the same programme**. In Germany, it was a pleasure to **enjoy watching together**, while in Ukraine the enjoyment of watching together and the interest in the same programmes contributed almost equally. In Latvia, in addition to these two reasons, the fact that respondents **do not have more televisions** was more pronounced, and this was a joint activity that could be partly enforced by circumstances.

In our survey, we have mapped only selected common media activities, of course the current technology allows much more (sharing photos, creating family videos, social networking activities, sharing music, etc.). There is a large number of opportunities for the positive use of modern digital technologies in family life and it is mainly a matter of creativity of the current parent generation, how they will approach these possibilities and whether they integrate them appropriately into their lifestyle and into educational strategies or not.

5.5   Different and Common Features of Family Lives with Media

Looking at our survey, data also raises a question of what common or different media traits we can see in family life. First, the characteristics of families in the countries of our survey are briefly summarized, and then their main common features and differences are outlined.

The Czech Republic proved to be a country with a high saturation rate of media, i.e. television, mobile phones with considerable access to the Internet, but at the time of our research tablets were lower represented in Czech families. Internet access was high (97.6%). In terms of the use of media by generations of parents or children, television and video players in the Czech Republic were more of a parental medium, while other media (except computers) were used more by children. In terms of daily use of media, Czech families reported television and computers and half of the respondents also reported tablets.[4] Roughly one third of respondents watches TV, video or DVD more than 2 hours a day, while 1% does not watch anything at all. The Czech Republic was one of the countries in which gaming was not so widespread. Most of Czech respondents agreed that the media facilitated communication and negotiation in their households and allowed respondents to be more independent (more than 50%). Positive aspects of media were therefore more perceived and the Eurobarometer survey also showed a higher share of trust in radio, television, the Internet and electronic social networks. One third of the surveyed households plays computer games at least occasionally at home and more than 90% watch TV at least occasionally together. Very common is watching TV together in about 43%. Czech households watch TV shows together mainly because they like the same programmes.

At the time of our research (data collection 2013–2014), **Latvian families** seemed to be entering a phase of higher mass media coverage of households. They showed a clearer share of families that did not have some of the devices (computers, DVD players, game consoles, IPods, MP3 players and tablets). At the same time, there was a slightly higher share of households that did not have a mobile phone. Internet access was almost 90%, but among the studied countries it was the lowest. On the other hand, in the Eurobarometer survey (2017), Latvian families have already shown, for example, significantly higher daily use of electronic social networks, but rather lower trust in the Internet and social networks. Also in our survey, despite the lower equipment of tablets, the studied families showed that those households who had them used them very intensively (63% of them used them every day). Similarly, Latvian families watched TV, videos and DVDs intensively. Almost 43% watched these devices over 2 hours per day. But they used TV less to watch TV programmes and used for it more the Internet. Latvian families have identified themselves most with the statement saying that the media allow them to pursue their own hobbies and entertainment and to facilitate communication. Compared to other countries, they expressed that they usually spend more time with the media than talking at

---

[4]Mobile phones are outside of this comparison as its everyday use was a matter of course.

home (almost 50% of households). At the same time, Latvia was a country where respondents reported frequent arguments because of the media (almost a quarter of respondents). Watching television together was quite often in Latvian families (47% very often, 47% occasionally). In the question: with whom do you watch television, video or DVD most often in your free time, respondents stated that they predominantly watch television, video or DVD alone (almost 95%). This was a significant difference from other countries. It brings a paradox that needs a further clarification. This may be also related, for example, to the understanding of both questions in the questionnaire.

German families were generally characterized by lower level of TV equipment (almost a quarter said that they do not have a TV set) and also by lower television use, which was probably offset by computer equipment that was also used to watch TV programmes.[5] The equipment of the other media devices was rather higher than in the other countries. Computers, televisions and surprisingly tablets were more of a parental media, while gaming consoles were used more by children. DVDs, video players and IPods + MP3 players roughly evenly intervened into both generations. In Germany, the daily use of media was also mostly connected with television and computer, about 1/3 of households used social networks every day (Eurobarometer). Germany was a country with a higher level of trust in radio, television and press, but with much lower trust in relation to the Internet and electronic social networks (there was the trust in these tools the lowest from all the analysed countries). PC and Internet gaming was rather smaller than in other countries. The German families were mostly in favour of the statement that the electronic media they have at home allow them to be independent and that the media facilitate communication. When compared to other countries, Germany belonged also among those countries where it was stressed more than anywhere else that the media distance family members away from each other. This rather individualizing aspect that we could observe in German families was confirmed games together.by watching TV together as a family or playing computer.

Poland was a country with relatively high media saturation of households; it even showed the highest Internet access (99%). At the same time, the Eurobarometer survey showed a higher level of trust in the Internet and electronic social networks (42% and 28%) in comparison to other countries. The trust was lower in traditional media such as radio, television and press. Television, video and DVD players were strong parental media in the Polish households, while computers, game consoles, IPods, Mp3 players and tablets were clearly used more by children. The daily use of selected media devices was rather lower, in terms of watching TV, videos, DVDs, and playing games on PC and on the Internet. Therefore, it is possible that overall the time devoted to media activities in Poland was lower than in other countries. In terms of attitudes towards the media, the Polish families have identified themselves most with the statement claiming that the media facilitate communication and allow

---

[5]For example, they used highly the Internet connection to watch the news (Eurobarometer).

them to pursue their hobbies and entertainment. Watching TV together as a family was quite common, gaming also appeared as an activity that family members do at least occasionally together.

Slovak families were well equipped with media devices at the time of the survey, with the exception of game consoles and tablets. In the Eurobarometer survey, Slovak respondents showed rather higher levels of trust in selected media and they watched television mainly through a TV set (not via the Internet). According to Eurobarometer, Slovakia was one of the countries with lower daily computer use (52%), but this was not reflected in the sample of our families. Slovakia reported more than 90% of daily computer and television use. However, substantially lower was a daily use of other media devices. In this respect, Slovak households have more traditional focus. As a daily leisure time activity, watching TV and computer use were represented in about 60% of respondents. In comparison to other countries, in Slovakia was recorded higher computer and Internet gaming, around 50% of households play games every day. However, it was rather an independent activity of respondents, not a joint playing of family members. On the other hand, watching television was more common activity of households. Slovak respondents of our research strongly inclined to the opinion that the electronic media they have facilitated their communication and negotiation. This was related to the fact that thanks to the media they could be more independent. Slovak families where those of all studied countries who also agreed the most to spend more time with the media than talking at home with other family members (53%).

Ukrainian households[6] were also relatively well equipped with the media, only gaming consoles in more than 3/4 of households were not present. In the Ukraine, television and computers were used extensively every day, as well as IPod, MP3 players, gaming consoles and mainly tablets. Tablets were also used in the most of the Ukrainian households, with almost three quarters of those who use these tablets every day. IPods, MP3 players, computers and tablets were more of a children's media, because more than 50% of them were used by children. In the Ukrainian households, there was also a higher frequency of computer games, 80% said that they were playing daily and almost 50% that it was even more than 2 hours a day. For the Ukrainian respondents, the media mainly meant that everyone could devote their time to hobbies and entertainment and that they could spend their free time together. However, almost 50% of respondents also reflected that they usually spend more time with the media than talking at home, and almost one quarter also reported frequent quarrels at home because of the media.

The families we studied had in common a considerable saturation of some media devices—computers, the Internet access, mobile phones and also TV sets. On the other hand, some of the devices have not been so common in the households (tablets, game consoles). Some of the recent digital devices showed differences at the time of our survey; for example, IPods and MP3 players were already present in most of the households in the Czech Republic, Germany, Slovakia and also in Ukraine, but in

---

[6]The Ukraine was not part of the Eurobarometer 88 survey; therefore, the data come only from our LSCF survey.

Latvia and Poland the prevailing part of households did not have them. Video players were widely represented in the Czech Republic and Slovakia, while in the other countries it did not occurred in most of the households. Televisions and computers were used mostly every day; this was same for all the countries. Differences were found mainly in the case of the daily use of tablets, IPods and MP3 players. Tablets were mostly used mainly in the Ukraine and Latvia, IPods and MP3 players every day in more than 50% of households, that owned them, in the Ukraine.

Overall, it can be stated that the media and media facilities are an essential part of the lives of contemporary families and that they have been well represented in households at the time of our survey. At the same time, the development in this area has progressed significantly in recent years and it can thus be assumed that the current modern digital means are also largely involved in the leisure time activities of family members. Some media activities are carried out in families together, some rather encourage individualization within family life. This is one of the reasons why the interviewed families point out the benefits that the media bring to their lives, that the media allow them to be more independent and that they also allow easy communication between family members and bring a way how to realize their hobbies and entertainment. Nevertheless, the media in some households are also a source of tension, conflict and distance family members from each other. However, these negative aspects did not the interviewed families highlighted as strongly as the apparent positives of the media.

References

Bartholomew, M. K., Schoppe-Sullivan, S. J., Glassman, M., Kamp Dush, C. M., & Sullivan, J. M. (2012). New parents' Facebook use at the transition to parenthood. *Family Relations*, *61*(3), 455–469. https://doi.org/10.1111/j.1741-3729.2012.00708.x

Broderick, C. B. (1993). *Understanding family process: Basics of family systems theory*. Thousand Oaks, CA: Sage.

Buermann, U. (2009). *Jak (pře)žít s médii*. Fabula: Hranice.

Coyne, S. M., Bushman, B. J., & Nathanson, A. I. (2012), Media and the family: A note from the guest editors. *Family Relations, 61*, s. 359–362.

Coyne, S. M., Padilla-Walker, L. M., Fraser, A. M., Fellows, K., & Day, R. D. (2014). Media time = family time: Positive media use in families with adolescents. *Journal of Acolescent Research, 29*(5), 1–26.

Czech Statistical Office. Informační společnost v číslech. (2019). https://www.czso.cz/csu/czso/inf ormacni-spolecnost-v-cislech-2018. Accessed 7 July 2019.

Dalope, K. A., & Woods, L. J. (2018). Digital media use in families: Theories and strategies for intervention. *Child and Adolescent Psychiatric Clinics of North America, 27*(2), 145–158.

Davies, J. J., & Gentile, D. A. (2012). Responses to childrens' media use in families with and without siblings: A family development perspective. *Family Relations, 61,* 410–425.

Eurobarometer. (2017). https://ec.europa.eu/commfrontoffice/publicopinion/index.cfm/Survey/get SurveyDetail/instruments/STANDARD/surveyKy/2143. Accessed 4 May 2018.

Gee, E., Cirell, A. M., & Siyahhan, S. (2017). Video gaming as digital media, play, and family routine: Implications for understanding video gaming and learning in family contexts. *Learning, Media and Technology, 42*(4), 468–482.

Gentile, D. A., & Walsh, D. (2002). A normative study of family media habits. *Applied Developmental Psychology, 23*(2), 157–178.

Geraghty, C. (1996). Representation and popular culture. *Mass Media and Society*, 265–279.

Gondová, K. (2014). *Výchovné problémy v současných rodinách spojené s používáním médií*. Hradec Králové: Univerzita Hradec Králové.

Green, K. M. (2008). *Understanding college students' and parents' perceptions of cell phone communication in family relationships: A grounded theory approach*. University of Minnesota.

Hagen, I. (2007). 'We can't just sit the whole day watching TV': Negotiations concerning media use among youngsters and their parents. *Young, 15*(4), 369–393.

Hertlein, K. M. (2012). Digital dwelling: Technology in couple and family relationships. *Family Relations, 61*(3), 374–387.

Hoover, S. M., Clark, L. S., & Alters, D. F. (2004). *Media, home and family*. New York: Routledge.

Jenkins, H., et al. (2009). *Confronting the challenges of participatory culture. Media education for the 21st century*. Cambridge, MA: MIT Press.

Jordan, A., et al. (2006). Reducing children's television-viewing time. A qualitative study of parents and their children. *Pediatrics, 18*, e1301–e1310.

Koerner, A. F., & Fitzpatrick, M. A. (2006). Family communication patterns theory: A social cognitive approach. In *Engaging theories in family communication: Multiple perspectives* (pp. 50–65). Thousand Oaks, CA: Sage.

Latvia. Statistics in Brief. (2019). https://www.csb.gov.lv/en/statistics/statistics-by-theme/eco nomy/gdp/search-in-theme/373-latvia-statistics-brief-2019. Accessed 8 July 2019.

Livingstone, S. (2002). *Young people and new media*. London: Sage.

Nathanson, A. I., & Manohar, U. (2012). The role of attachment in college students' working models of parenting and expectations for using television in child rearing. *Family Relations, 61*, 441–454.

Nikken, P. (2017). Implications of low or high media use among parents for young children's media use. *Cyberpsychology-Journal of Psychosocial Research on Cyberspace, 11*(3).

Padilla-Walker, L. M., Coyne, S. M., Fraser, A. M. (2012). Getting a high-speed family connection? Associations between family media use and family connection. Family Relations, 61 426–440.

Reeves, B., & Nass, C. (1998). *The media equation*. Cambridge: Center for the Study of Language and Information.

Roberts, D. F., & Foehr, U. G. (2008). Trends in media use. *Future of Children, 18*(1), 11–37.

Sak, P., & Kolesárová, K. (2004). *Mládež na křižovatce: sociologická analýza postavení mládeže ve společnosti a její úlohy v procesech evropeizace a informatizace*. Praha: Svoboda Servis.

Stašová, L., Junová, I., & Adámková, T., (2012). Electronic media in the environment of the contemporary households and families. *Educational Technologies (EDUTE 2012): Proceedings of the 8th WSEAS International Conference. Athens: World Scientific and Engineering Academy and Society* (pp. 111–116).

Šeďová, K. (2007). *Děti a rodiče pied televizí: rodinná socializace dětského televizního diváctví*. Brno: Paido.

Takeuchi, L. M. (2011). *Families matte: Designing media for a digital age*. New York: The Joan Ganz Conney Center.

Taylor, K. H., Takeuchi, L., & Stevens, R. (2018). Mapping the daily media round: novel methods for understanding families' mobile technology use. *Learning Media and Technology, 43*(1), 70–84.

Tobias, S. (2017). Predicting video game play from perceived family environment among university students. *Journal of Family Studies, 23*(2), 215–227.

Torrecillas-Lacave, T., Vyzquez-Barrio, T., & Monteagudo-Barandalla, L. (2017). The perception of parents about the digital empowerment of family in hyperconnected households. *Profesional de la Informacion, 26*(1), 97–104.

Turkle, S. (2011). *Alone together*. New York: Basic Books.

Ünal, S. (2018). The effect of social media use to the time spent with family members. *International Journal of Eurasia Social Sciences, 9*(31), 550–578.

Vanderwater, E. A., Bickham, D. S., Lee, J. H., Cummings, H. M., Wartella, E. A., & Rideout, V. J. (2005). When the television is always on: heavy television exposure and young children's development. *American Behavioral Scientist, 48*(5), 562–577.

Vittrup, B., Snider, S., Rose, K. K., & Rippy, J. (2016). Parental perceptions of the role of media and technology in their young children's lives. *Journal of Early Childhood Research, 14*(1), 43–54.

Watkins, S. C. (2009). *The young & the digital.* Boston: Beacon Press.

Weisskirch, R. S. (2009). Parenting by cell phone. Parental monitoring of adolescents and family relations. *Journal of Youth and Adolescence, 38,* 1123–1139.

Wenhold, H., & Harrison, K. (2018). Television use and family mealtimes among a sample of US families with preschoolers. *Journal of Children, 12*(1), 98–115. https://doi.org/10.1080/174 82798.2017.1395751

Yu, X., Anaya, G. J., Miao, L., Lehto, X., & Wong, I. A. (2018). The Impact of smartphones on the family vacation experience. *Journal of Travel Research, 57*(5), 579–596. https://doi.org/10. 1177/0047287517706263. ISSN 00472875. Accessed 15 April 2019.

Zabriskie, R. B., & McCormick, B. P. (2001). The influences of family leisure patterns on perceptions of family functioning. *Family Relations, 50,* 281–289.

Conclusion

Family represents topic that is extremely serious and up to date. Is has undergone significant changes as never before over the last decades. Despite all these changes, which has undergone, it remains primary educational institution and primary social environment. All this complexity we have tried to show in this publication, how difficult it is to deal with traditional functions, how standard of living is influenced by the contemporary society, how actually the contemporary family looks like and lives. Both on the basis of all available expert knowledge from not only sources, but also from confrontations with foreign ones, based on several surveys and mainly above all our research.

In the introductory chapter, we present two basic categories of the whole monograph: the family and the way of living. There is a description of the post-war family development in Europe until now, differentiated in the Western and Eastern part. It turns out that changes in the society have caused significant changes also in the family lives. Furthermore, we explain the term lifestyle and its different concepts, ways of lifestyle and its types according to various aspects. At present, the concept of healthy lifestyle and its shaping plays a highly significant role.

In the review study, there are several surveys which deal with family lives (e.g. Maříková 1999, Chaloupková 2005, Kraus and Jedličková 2007, Višňovský et al. 2010, Holubová 2011). They relate to roles in the family and their changes, division of work, household work, public view at marriage and parenthood, parents' needs, issues in the family and time budget. In the conclusion of the whole chapter, there is project of our survey, its goals, methods, research sample (total of 2437 respondents) and the survey process. The research team set a goal to monitor family lifestyle in four fields: socioeconomic situation, life satisfaction, leisure time and ways of spending it and media in a family, its use and attitudes towards its role in the family lives.

The contemporary family is more likely in all countries somehow marked by advancing democratization, social differentiation, disintegration and by unemployment to varying degrees, certain isolation and intergenerational relationships passes through certain changes as well.

Authors also pay attention to family social policy, housing situation when starting a family, the fact, that in individual countries is done by the society. Also, an increase

© The Editor(s) (if applicable) and The Author(s) 2020
B. Kraus et al., *Contemporary Family Lifestyles in Central and Western Europe*,
SpringerBriefs in Sociology, https://doi.org/10.1007/978-3-030-48299-2

in violence as well as differences in family lives living in towns or in the country side is stated. The image of a German family, unlike other countries, is marked by strong migration wave.

The social economic situation seems to be a big current issue. Tomu je věnována následující kapitola. This is documented in the international research, monitoring life conditions in households in the Czech Republic, Poland, Hungary and Slovakia and are confirmed by the results of our international research. We are interested in the income situation, expenditure items, experience with unemployment and respondents were also to evaluate their overall standard of living. The Germans and then the Czech respondents evaluate their situation as the best. The worst perception is given by families from Latvia.

We also monitored the overall life satisfaction. According to the respondents, it is represented by harmony living without conflicts, well-being, good health of all family members and material security without major differences shown among monitored countries. On the other hand, the differences were found in cases where respondents had to state what they lack to satisfaction. Most often, it was financial security and the lack of free time for the family.

Historical context and changes are described in the chapter about leisure time in terms of amount and ways of spending leisure time. The importance of leisure time has gradually increased for individuals and also for the society. The current leisure time is no longer perceived quantitatively (such as time, that is left), but based on its quality, such as time of freedom, recreation and self-realization. It fulfils several important functions for the human. In most surveyed countries, the lack of mutually spent leisure time with the family was perceived as the most important issue that hinders family satisfaction. In terms of the amount of leisure time, the most satisfied respondents come from Latvia and the Czech Republic. In these countries, the leisure time outweighs the standard working week, weekends and holidays. On the contrary, the least satisfied with the amount of free time are respondents from Poland. In terms of quality of spending of leisure time, the function of relax is essential for working respondents. It is evaluated in a positive way. The number of respondents who are satisfied with the quality of relax in their free time outweighs significantly. But this is no longer true for the satisfaction of the time of their interests. The respondents would like to make more trips, travel, do more sport, social games and fun with their families. They are most often prevented from two reasons—lack of time and finance. Reading and watching television are dominant leisure time activities of individual respondents. Whereas reading is clearly individual activity, watching television is an activity that is shared by family members. Other leisure activities in which the whole family participates are gardening, visiting friends and relatives, visits of cultural events, walks and board games.

At the time of the research, the households in the surveyed countries were already saturated with electronic media. Families with children are generally the types of households that obtain new technologies quickly and use them. They often get new media tools because of children and to use them for school preparation in order to "keep up with" their peer groups. The families were very well equipped with computers, mobile phones, televisions and also had the Internet access. On the other hand, some tools were being found in households (e.g. game console or IPod and MP3 players mainly in Latvia and the Ukraine). What, was possible to observe at the same time in our data, was a certain "generational differentiation" of media, and who uses them at home most often. For example, while the television was dominant parent medium, then tables, game consoles, IPod and MP3 players were used by children to a much greater extend.

Media activities were among relatively frequent activities of leisure time members of the survey families. Especially, watching television and computer activities belonged to what the families do every day. Watching TV together was then favourite activity of a large part of Slovakian, Polish and Latvian households. Family members point out both benefits and negatives as well what media brings to them. All in all, they point out more positives brought by the media. They perceive media device as a way of easier communication, independence in order to pursue hobbies and fun.

In our research, there were included five countries of the former Eastern block of countries and one from the Western part. In many aspects of family lives, it was possible to distinguish differences between both groups. On contrary, there were found also dissimilarities among individual countries. We hope that our data can mirror very interesting features of lifestyles in studied countries and show the lived diversity in Europe.

The investigation is carried out within the project "Development and support of a multidisciplinary scientific research team for studying the current family at UHK" - CZ. 1.07/2.3.00/20.0209. This publication is supported by the Faculty of Education, University of Hradec Králové.

Appendix

Questionnaire

We would like to ask you to complete an anonymous questionnaire focused on the quality of life of contemporary families. Its completion is not time consuming—should not take more than 20 minutes. Please tick with a cross x chosen possibility. For items where are more possibilities given tick all of them which you prefer. For items where an answer is necessary to be completed—just write down your opinion very briefly.

© The Editor(s) (if applicable) and The Author(s) 2020   115
B. Kraus et al., *Contemporary Family Lifestyles in Central and Western Europe*,
SpringerBriefs in Sociology, https://doi.org/10.1007/978-3-030-48299-2

1. Permanently live in :

☐ a municipality with population less than 1000

☐ a municipality with population 1000–5000

☐ a municipality with population 5–10000

☐ older town buildings with population 10000–20000

☐ older town buildings with population 20000–100000

☐ older town buildings with population over 100000

☐ a housing estate with population 10000–20000

☐ a housing estate with population 20000–100000

☐ a housing estate with population over 100000

☐ a new development with family houses on the outskirts with population 10000–20000

☐ a new development with family houses on the outskirts with population 20000–100000

☐ a new development with family houses on the outskirts with population over 100000

2. Number of children *(in the family – write):* ....

3. Year of birth: husband ....   wife ....

4. Occupation (*write):* husband .... wife....................................

5. The highest level of education:

	Primary	Trained	Secondary	Higher education	College
Husband					
Wife					

6. The major income for your family is:

☐ income from employment ☐ income from social benefits ☐ other income *(list what)*
… … … … … … ….

7. Who from your family makes own economic activity (in employment)?

☐ both parents ☐ one parent ☐ parents and children ☐ nobody

8. Who from your family makes the highest expenditure items? *(write down):*

… …

… …

9. Do you get as a family some of the state social benefits or a batch of material need?

☐ YES ☐ NO

10. Do you have experience with unemployment? ☐ YES ☐ NO

11. Do you have possibility to save something from your monthly finance means (make a reserve)?

☐ YES ☐ NO

12. How do you rate yourself your standard of living?

☐ very bad ☐ rather bad ☐ average ☐ rather good ☐ very good

13. How do you imagine a happy family? (*write down):*

… …

… …

14. What do you miss in family satisfaction? (*write down):*

… …

… …

15. Express yourself to the satisfaction with the quantity and quality of the free time.

	1	2	3	4	5	6	7
	Very satisfied	Not satisfied	Rather dissatisfied	Yes dissatisfied, neither satisfied	Rather satisfied	Satisfied	Very satisfied
With the quantity of free time after work I am							
With the quantity of free time during the weekend I am							
With the length of yearly leave I am							
With the quality of rest which I get during my holiday I am							
With the quality of rest I have in my free time I am							
With the quality of free time which I have for my hobbies I am							
With the quantity of free time which I can be with my loved ones I am							
With diversity of my free time I am							

16. What activities would you like to do in your free time?

……

……

17. Do you play sometimes together PC games at home?

☐ YES, very often   ☐ YES, occasionally   ☐ NO, never

18. Do you do any sport in your free time?   ☐ YES   ☐ NO

19. If you do sport, what sport do you do? How often and which of them do you do together with a family member? *(write down and please tick the box with the suitable answer.*

Write down the type of sport-physical activity	How often do you do it				With whom		
	daily	3-4x a week	1-2x a week	less frequently	alone	with wife	with children

20. Define the scope of your daily free time in hours:

Husband:

☐ I never have free time

☐ I have free time only during public holiday, weekends

☐ less than a 1 hour daily

☐ 1 hour daily

☐ 2 hours daily

☐ 3 hours daily

☐ 4 hours daily

☐ 5 hours daily

☐ 6 and more hours daily

☐ depends on a season (indicate closer):
....
....

Wife:

☐ I never have free time

☐ I have fee time only during public holiday, weekends

☐ less than a 1 hour daily

☐ 1 hour daily

☐ 2 hours daily

☐ 3 hours daily

☐ 4 hours daily

☐ 5 hours daily

☐ 6 and more hours daily

☐ depends on a season (indicate closer):
....
....

21. Each of us assumes some areas in the life that are more important than others and tries to seek for achievement. Which areas you consider to prefer in your family – put into order according to your importance from the most important "1" to less important "9" *fill in number into the boxes).*

☐ Good and interesting work

☐ Healthy, safe environment

☐ Happy family life

☐ High standard of living (enough money)

☐ Health

☐ Helping others, work for others

☐ Free time spent together

☐ Personal character, moral qualities

☐ Others *(write):* ... ...

22. What leisure activities are typical for you? You can list up to 5 answers. *In case of chosen activity please list who you do it with.*

Leisure activity	We often do activity			Leisure activity	I often do activity		
	alone	with a family member	With friends		alone	with a family member	with friends
I have no				Watching TV			
Reading				Listening to music (at home)			
Music performance (playing a musical instrument, signing)				Entertainment venues visits (disco, wine cellars, restaurant			
Concerts				Visits, Narration, inviting friends			
Theatre going				Walks, trips			
Cinema going				Sport activities			
Handicraft				Chess, billiard, board games			
Do-it-yourself				Clubs – write down:			
Work in the garden				Others (write):			

23. What types of electronic media do you have in your household and what number?

(list the number of each media)

	Number of pcs
a TV	
a computer	
a DSVD player	
a video player	

	Number of pcs
a game console	
iPod, mp3	
a tablet	
a mobile phone	

	YES	NO
Internet access		

24. Who from your family uses this equipment the most? *(please tick the box with x)*

	Somebody from parents	Somebody from children	Somebody else
a TV			
a PC			
a DVD player			
a video player			
a game console			
iPod, mp3			
a tablet			

	Every day	Several times a week	Max. once a week	Less frequently
a TV				
a PC				
a DVD player				
a video player				
a game console				
iPod, mp3				
a tablet				

26. To what extent to you agree with these following statements? *(please tick the box with x)*

	very agree	rather agree	rather disagree	strongly disagree
Electronic media which we have at home make our communication and agreement easier				
We often argue at home because of (a TV, a PC and other)				
Media as good means of meeting and spending time together				
Home media cut the relationship within the family				
Electronic media that we have at home allow us to be independent				
Most time we spend by the media (a TV, a PC and other) than by talking to each other at home				
If we did not have media at home (a TV, a PC and other), we would have lived better				
Media that we have at home allow us to turn to our own hobbies and fun				

27. Do you sometimes watch TV together?

☐ YES, very often ☐ YES, occasionally ☐ NO, never

28. If yes, what type of TV program do you usually watch together? *(write down)*

… …

… …

29. What is the main reason that you watch TV together?

☐ We have no more other televisions, there is no other way.

☐ We like the same programme so we watch it together.

☐ We like to watch together; therefore we choose the same program.

☐ From other reason *(write):* ………………………………………………………………………..

30. How often in your free time do you spend these following activities?

	more than 2 hours a day	Less than 2 hours a day	several times a week	once a week	several times a month	once a month	several times a year	not a bit	do not know	individually	with sb from a family
Reading books, magazines											
Studying (languages, self-education, …)											
Sport activities, exercise (active regular exercise)											
Hiking, trips											
Theatre, exhibitions, …											
Visit cafés, restaurants, …											
Watching TV, video, DVD, …											
PC games, internet											
Household work, garden work											
Passive recreation, idleness											
Meeting with relatives, friends											
Child care (games, learning, ….)											
Self-care (beauty salon, solarium, etc.)											
Others…											

31. If you have something to say, to add to the investigation *(write down)*

… …

… …

… …

For the team of investigators—thank you for your time and willingness while completing the questionnaire!